ADVANCE PRAISE FOR
Derrida, Deconstruction, AND THE Politics OF Pedagogy

"Michael A. Peters' and Gert Biesta's book first explores Derrida's philosophy in the eyes of foes and friends. It then follows a nuanced and generously humane analysis of key concepts in Derrida's work in their bearing on politics and education today. The transparent text guides the reader towards a well-argued view for a different future for general education in a time of its much-needed renewal. This is a rare and well-written book and a fine contribution to the philosophy of education by two of its expert scholars."

Lars Løvlie, Professor of Philosophy of Education,
Institute for Educational Research, University of Oslo

Derrida, Deconstruction,
AND THE Politics OF Pedagogy

Studies in the
Postmodern Theory of Education

Joe L. Kincheloe and Shirley R. Steinberg
General Editors

Vol. 323

PETER LANG
New York • Washington, D.C./Baltimore • Bern
Frankfurt am Main • Berlin • Brussels • Vienna • Oxford

MICHAEL A. PETERS and GERT BIESTA

Derrida, Deconstruction, AND THE Politics OF Pedagogy

PETER LANG
New York • Washington, D.C./Baltimore • Bern
Frankfurt am Main • Berlin • Brussels • Vienna • Oxford

Library of Congress Cataloging-in-Publication Data
Peters, Michael A.
Derrida, deconstruction, and the politics of pedagogy /
Michael A. Peters, Gert Biesta.
p. cm. — (Counterpoints: studies in the postmodern theory
of education; v. 323)
Includes bibliographical references and index.
1. Derrida, Jacques. 2. Deconstruction. 3. Education.
I. Biesta, Gert. II. Title.
B2430.D484P47   194—dc22   2008043974
ISBN 978-1-4331-0009-3
ISSN 1058-1634

Bibliographic information published by **Die Deutsche Bibliothek**.
Die Deutsche Bibliothek lists this publication in the "Deutsche
Nationalbibliografie"; detailed bibliographic data is available
on the Internet at http://dnb.ddb.de/.

© 2009 Peter Lang Publishing, Inc., New York
29 Broadway, 18th floor, New York, NY 10006
www.peterlang.com

All rights reserved.
Reprint or reproduction, even partially, in all forms such as microfilm,
xerography, microfiche, microcard, and offset strictly prohibited.

TABLE OF CONTENTS

Acknowledgments   vii

Introduction: The Promise of Politics and Pedagogy   1
Michael A. Peters and Gert Biesta

Chapter 1   Deconstruction, Justice, and the
Vocation of Education   15
Gert Biesta

Chapter 2   Derrida as a Profound Humanist   39
Michael A. Peters

Chapter 3   Derrida, Nietzsche, and the Return to the Subject   59
Michael A. Peters

Chapter 4   From Critique to Deconstruction: Derrida as a
Critical Philosopher   81
Gert Biesta

Chapter 5	Education after Deconstruction: Between Event and Invention Gert Biesta	97
Chapter 6	The University and the Future of the Humanities Michael A. Peters	115
	Welcome! Postscript on Hospitality, Cosmopolitanism, and the Other Michael A. Peters	133
	Index	139

ACKNOWLEDGMENTS

For Michael A. Peters

The Introduction "The Promise of Politics and Pedagogy" is a version of "The Promise of Politics and Pedagogy in Derrida," *The Review of Education/Pedagogy/Cultural Studies*, 28(2) (April–June 2006): 123–139 (17). Chapter 3 is based on part of the Introduction taken and modified from Peters, M.A. (ed.), *Naming the Multiple: Poststructuralism and Education*, Westport, CT. & London, Bergin & Garvey, (1998). Chapter 6 is based on "The University and the New Humanities: Professing with Derrida," *Arts and Humanities in Higher Education* 3(1): 41–57 (2003). "Welcome! Postscript on Hospitality, Cosmopolitanism; and the Other" is based on a section of an unpublished paper "Cultural Exchange, Study Abroad and the Discourse of the Other" by Michael A Peters and Shivali Tukdeo.

For Gert Biesta

Chapter 1 is partly based on Biesta, G.J.J. (1998). Deconstruction, justice and the question of education. *Zeitschrift für Erziehungswissenschaft*, 1(3): 395–411 and Chapter 4 on Biesta, G.J.J. & Stams, G.J.J.M. (2001). Critical thinking and the question of critique. Some lessons from deconstruction. *Studies in Philosophy and*

Education, 20(1): 57–74. For Chapter 5 material has been used from Biesta, G.J.J. (2004). Education after deconstruction. In J. Marshall (ed.), *Poststructuralism, Philosophy, Pedagogy* (pp. 27–42). Dordrecht/Boston: Kluwer Academic Press.

EWALD: Is there a philosophy of Jacques Derrida?
DERRIDA: No.
EWALD: Therefore there is no message?
DERRIDA: No message.
EWALD: Is there any normativity?
DERRIDA: Of course there is, that's all there is.

(Derrida & Ewald, 1995: 289)

INTRODUCTION: THE PROMISE OF POLITICS AND PEDAGOGY

MICHAEL A. PETERS AND GERT BIESTA

Derrida's death on Friday the 8th of October 2004 spawned the same journalistic insouciance and caustic xenophobia on both sides of the Atlantic that occasioned his work when he was alive. The *New York Times* published a scurrilous front-page obituary with the headline "Jacques Derrida, Abstruse Theorist, Dies in Paris at 74," written by Jonathan Kandell that recalled the culture wars of the 1980s and prompted outrage from his American "friends." Kandell, refueling the "de Man affair" and emphasizing Heidegger's influence on Derrida's thought, poured scorn on deconstruction and revived the conservative critique mounted by the likes of Roger Kimball and Allan Bloom. Samuel Weber and Kenneth Reinhard responded by describing Kandell's obituary as "mean-spirited and uninformed" and went on to argue that far from "undermining many of the traditional standards of classical education," as Kandell maintained, Derrida in fact "wrestled with central works of the Western tradition, including Plato, Shakespeare, and the Declaration of Independence—none of which he slighted." They sparked an avalanche: their joint letter gathered so many signatures that the School of Humanities at the University of California, Irvine, where he had taught for many years, hosted a memorial web site.[1] The letter from UCI faculty, students, and staff to the *New York Times* accused Kandell of "shabbily misrepresent[ing] the life and achievements of a great thinker, a most generous teacher, and a courteous human being." The letter goes on to list the eleven honorary degrees and other honors bestowed upon Derrida, as well as the 70 books he wrote and the 420 speaking engagements he gave over forty years of active service around the globe. It also quashed the rumor that at Irvine he was paid "hefty fees."

Karen Lawrence and Andrzej Warminski's (dean of humanities and head of English at UCI) joint statement speaks palpably and unambiguously as a testament to Derrida foremost as a teacher. It is important to quote this in full:

> Those who know "Derrida" only as the world's most famous contemporary philosopher or as an international "celebrity" might be surprised to learn that his teaching activity made an invaluable and indelible contribution to the intellectual life of UCI. Starting in 1987, he taught a regular seminar in the spring quarter that, for five weeks, consisted of two two-hour lectures open to the public and one two-hour discussion session for the graduate students enrolled in the course for credit. The opening lectures of each seminar would usually draw a crowd of around 150 students and faculty, as well as some curiosity seekers, from all over California. This number would settle down to 80 or so serious participants once it quickly became clear that the seminar was not going to be just a spectacle but rather a rigorous inquiry into a difficult (and often timely) topic. But however difficult the problem addressed and however rigorous Derrida's working through it, evident to all was Derrida's genuine pedagogical gift. A true "philosopher" in the ancient Greek sense, Derrida was always, and first of all, a teacher.
>
> However, Derrida's pedagogy was not confined to classroom instruction. He generously served on graduate students' Ph.D. qualifying examinations, turning them into intellectual events. Always unstinting in his praise of good work, Derrida would never fail to point out, delicately and politely, what the student (or the faculty member serving on the committee!) had not yet thought through, how he or she could and should go further and ask more questions before hurrying to premature answers. Equally generous and equally unsparing, Derrida's extensive comments on students' papers became collectors' items. They arrived in the summer in the form of two- or three- or four-page letters written by hand in Derrida's distinctive hand-writing. Derrida's dedication to his teaching was also clear in the six hours (and more) a week he devoted to office hours. Every Monday, Tuesday, and Wednesday a passerby would see a line of students outside the door of Derrida's office in Humanities Hall—with every student getting the time needed to discuss his or her paper topic.

The allusion to Socrates and the Socratic tradition has been mentioned by a number of commentators, who, in addition, have written powerfully of Derrida in relation to the Socratic vocation of philosophy as a kind of dying, linking him not only to trumped-up charges about the corruption of youth, but also to the trope on "the death of the author," *hauntology*, ghosts, and specters. For Derrida, who actively explored death and deconstruction as the work of mourning and, following Heidegger and Levinas, held that giving one's life for the other is the purest demonstration of individuality. In *The Gift of Death*—which was originally presented at Royaumont, in December 1990, in a conference entitled "The Ethics of the Gift"—Derrida explored self-sacrifice as grounded upon its status as a radically individualistic gift. Here the notion of the gift is an ineffable horizon that conditions political, philosophical, ethical, and religious tradition and yet transcends all conceptualization. Some of Derrida's most powerful meditations on friends and colleagues who were his contemporaries, such as Foucault, Levinas, de Man, Deleuze, and Lyotard, come down to us in the form of eulogies and memorials. This "attitude towards death" was also to elicit cheap jokes. John J. Miller and Mark Molesky, writing in *The National Review*, began their piece with the following one-liner: "It is tempting to say that Jacques Derrida's death has been greatly exaggerated. The French philosopher was so closely associated with nihilism and metaphysical absence that it's perhaps worth wondering whether he ever lived at all."[2]

Derrida's death was received in the UK in very similar ways. It was almost a replay. Roger Scruton dismissed Derrida as an "anything goes" philosopher and *The Times* claimed that Derrida "carried on the demolition [of objective truth and traditional morality] where Nietzsche left off." *The Economist* (October 21, 2004) wrote: "The inventor of deconstruction—an ill-defined habit of dismantling texts by revealing their assumptions and contradictions—was indeed, and unfortunately, one of the most cited modern scholars in the humanities." It was up to Terry Eagleton, writing in *The Guardian* (October 15, 2004) with characteristic gusto, to bemoan "English philistinism" suggesting, "our home-grown intelligentsia gave a set of bemused, bone-headed responses to the death of Jacques Derrida. Either they hadn't read him, or they believed his work was to do with words not meaning what you think they do. Or it was just a pile of garbage." And he went on to say:

> The man was regarded by the stuffed shirts as a subversive nihilist who believed that words could mean anything you liked, that truth was a fiction, and that there was nothing in the world but writing. In their eyes, he was a dangerous mixture of anarchist, poet and jester. ...He was one of a lineage of anti-philosophers, from Kierkegaard to Wittgenstein, who invented a new style of philosophical writing. He understood that official thought turns on rigorously exclusive oppositions: inside/outside, man/woman, good/evil. He loosened up such paranoid antitheses by the flair and brio of his writing, and in doing so spoke up for the voiceless, from whose ranks he had emerged.

In media spaces, the bloggers were stretched for comment too. Where one blogger more cautiously ended his largely acrimonious posting with "I regret Derrida's death. I welcome the death of deconstructionism"; another clearly displayed his bias and anger—"Pretentious Asshole: Carefully Crafted Trashademic Thoughts."³ Rather poignantly and insightfully *Bat020* wrote:

> Derrida's death comes at a time when the constant ritual denunciations of his work have taken on a particularly ugly and strident tone. It is not difficult to see why. His patient, unyielding disassembly of the "white mythology" of Western metaphysics was bound to enrage our contemporary crusaders, those who would wish to squander the legacy of the European enlightenment by pressing it into the service of an obnoxious triumphalist imperial ideology. (http://bat.blogspot.com/)

Perhaps, most perceptively, Rachel Nigro (2005) in "Derrida's Last Conference" wrote with great precision, rising above the mire to comment on the symptoms of the discourse surrounding Derrida's death.

> Philosophy, strictly speaking, has been resistant to Derrida. This is a sign or a symptom that should be analyzed. Such rejection can be seen as a symptom of a disease that has been contaminating all manner of western academic discourse. There is a resistence [sic] to what is new, to what is unknown; the bureaucracy of thought that threatens all kinds of institutions and confines the capacity of thought in our time. This is what Derrida calls closure.

Nigro is right enough about this to hint at an epidemiology of Western philosophy.[4] This was evident in the so-called Cambridge affair as well, on the occasion of Derrida being awarded an honorary doctorate.

In May 1992, some twenty analytic philosophers from ten countries wrote a letter to the editor of *The Times* (published May 9) to protest and to intervene in a debate that occurred at Cambridge University over whether Jacques Derrida should be allowed to receive an honorary degree.[5] The signatories, none of whom were faculty at Cambridge, laid two very serious charges against Derrida: that his work "does not meet accepted standards of clarity and rigour" and that he is not a philosopher. In elaborating these two charges, they argued, first, that, although Derrida has shown "considerable originality" (based upon a number of "tricks" and "gimmicks"), he has, at the same time, stretched "the normal forms of academic scholarship beyond recognition," employed "a written style that defies comprehension," brought contemporary French philosophy into disrepute, and offered nothing but assertions that are either "false or trivial" in a series of "attacks upon the values of reason, truth and scholarship.[6] Second, they submitted, the fact that the influence of his work has been "almost entirely in fields outside philosophy" was sufficient grounds for casting doubt on his suitability as a candidate for an honorary degree in philosophy. This affair constitutes an event of some significance for it is unusual for philosophers from outside a university to attempt to interfere in the internal affairs of another by organizing opposition to the granting of an honorary degree through the news media.

What Derrida called "the Cambridge Affair" demonstrates the extent to which questions of style are at center stage in contemporary philosophy and how battle lines have been drawn over the issue of philosophy as both a form of discourse and a kind of writing.[7] On one side are a group of prominent and, indeed, internationally well-respected analytic philosophers who, in their joint attack upon Derrida, want to occlude questions of style. Driven by a conception of "scientific" philosophy wedded to a distinct method of analyticity, they are deeply concerned for the future of their discipline. The possibility that the institution of modern philosophy might come to accept as important the notion of style in philosophical writing, for them, leaves open the door to the enemies of rigor and clarity: persuasion, rhetoric, and metaphor.

Derrida's (1992b: 134) response to "the Cambridge Affair" was to focus upon the "journalistic" style of the letter itself and to understand it as "another demonstration of [philosophical] nationalism" that violates the very principles of "reason, truth and scholarship" that it claims to represent. He suggests that his inquisitors "confuse philosophy with what they have been taught to *reproduce* in the tradition and style of a particular institution" (135); in response to a question concerning the Parisian location of his own work, he comments: "One never writes just anywhere, out of a context and without trying to aim or privilege a certain readership, even if one can't and shouldn't limit oneself to this" (137). Perhaps, more than any philosopher before him, and from his earliest beginnings,[8] Derrida (1995: 218) has called attention to the *form* of "philosophical discourse"—its "modes of composition, its rhetoric, its metaphors, its language, its fictions" (218)—not in order to assimilate philosophy to literature but rather to recognize the complex links between the two and to investigate the ways in which the institutional authority of academic philosophy and the autonomy it claims rest upon a "disavowal with relation to its own language." The question of philosophical styles, he maintains, is, itself, a philosophical question (see also Peters & Burbules in Peters & Marshall, 1999).

Derrida as a Political Philosopher

The misunderstanding of Derrida goes deeper than that evidenced over the politics of his untimely death. Surprisingly, the Left has castigated him for his *lack* of politics. We have never been able to understand the claim made periodically over the last thirty years, particularly by members of the liberal and Marxist Left and by the likes of Jürgen Habermas, Thomas McCarthy, and Richard Rorty, that Jacques Derrida is not "political," or that deconstruction is agnostic, politically speaking. In our view Derrida is not only a political philosopher but perhaps even the most political of all contemporary philosophers. How can it be that such claims have been made against a philosopher who has been responsible for unhinging Western metaphysics and instituting a generalized critique of the Western "ideology" of presence? How can those who wish for a social democratic politics ignore "the political" in Derrida's critique of "logocentrism" and "phallocentrism"?

Habermas (1981) in his "Modernity versus Postmodernity" called Derrida a "Young Conservative" and accused him of recapitulating the experience of aesthetic modernity by decentering subjectivity and juxtaposing to instrumental reason a principle accessible only through a form of evocation. Later, Habermas (1987: 166–167) claimed that Derrida's "attempt to go beyond Heidegger does not escape the *aporetic* structure of a truth-occurrence eviscerated of all truth-as-validity." He maintains that the Nietzsche-inspired critique of the Western *logos* proceeds destructively and eventually collapses in upon itself: "It demonstrates that the embodied, speaking and acting subject is not master in its own house" (Habermas, 1987: 310) and, therefore, cannot be comfortably the basis of social democratic politics.

Richard Rorty (1997), while sympathetic to Derrida, sides with Habermas in wanting to preserve the Enlightenment's political project. Specifically, he wants to deny that there are any political implications that flow from the "new philosophical world-view" that emerges in the work of what he terms the neo-Nietzschean philosophers—Heidegger, Derrida, and Foucault (p. 36). This is a view that he formulates in the early 1990s and is worth repeating in the following lengthy quotation.

> The difference between these two varieties of post-Socratism—post-Emersonian American thought and post-Nietzschean European thought—can perhaps best be expressed as the difference between an attempt to disjoin art from politics and an attempt to assimilate the two. American intellectuals in the tradition of Emerson and James have thought of the task of fashioning a pluralistic and egalitarian society as something quite different from the pursuit of greatness. The only sense in which they think of a utopian society as a work of art is that they think of it as a merely human creation, not modelled on anything greater than the human. They have, if you like, given up on greatness, and on the transvaluation of all values. They have given up on

apocalyptic or eschatological rhetoric. In Europe, on the other hand, the influence of Heidegger, and in particular Heidegger's attempt to out-Nietzsche Nietzsche, has kept such rhetoric alive. (Rorty, 1991: 63)

Rorty divides off the philosophical and political projects of the Enlightenment to argue that abandoning Western rationalism has no discouraging political implications. The rejection of what Derrida calls "the metaphysics of presence," for Rorty, carries no political implications. He thinks we have no reason for abandoning the Enlightenment political project unless we can dream up a better one, unless we can articulate "an even better utopia," and, accordingly, he castigates the "principled, theorized, philosophical hopelessness" of the Nietzschean Left (Rorty, 1998a: 37). This is a view he develops most stridently in *Achieving Our Country* (Rorty, 1998a) aimed at the American "cultural left" who he alleges have chosen to embrace "apocalyptic French and German philosophy." Based upon this "resigned," "pessimistic," "spectatorial," "abstract," "over-theorized," and "over-philosophized" system-critique, Rory maintains, the cultural left, have substituted philosophy for political economy, and sadism (Freud) for selfishness (Marx).

Rorty is unkind to Derrida. Although he makes brief mention of Derrida's more recent work concerning "responsibility," like many other commentators he virtually ignores Derrida's recent political works and only once acknowledges the romantic utopian element in his work (see Rorty, 1998b: 138). Rorty does not, for instance, mention or consider Derrida's overtly political work in relation to: the institution of the university (e.g., Derrida, 1983a, 1984, 1989, 1992a), racism (e.g., Derrida, 1985), literature (e.g., Derrida, 1986b), law (e.g., Derrida, 1986a, 1990), linguistic and cultural identity (Derrida, 1998), and philosophy itself (e.g., Derrida, 1988). Nor does he consider Derrida's specific works on politics, most notably, *The Other Heading: Reflections on Today's Europe* (Derrida, 1992c), *Specters of Marx* (Derrida, 1994), and *Politics of Friendship* (Derrida, 1997a, b). He does, however, lend a sympathetic ear to deconstruction and he tries to understand its political implications as a critical practice.

> The present close association between radical politics and deconstructive literary criticism is the principal effect of this attempt by philosophers to put language in the place formerly occupied by Man.... Those who practice deconstructive criticism typically see themselves as taking part in an activity which has more to do with political change than with the "understanding" (much less than the "appreciation") of what has traditionally been called "literature." (Rorty, 1998b: 193)

Rorty goes on to suggest that the term "deconstruction" serves as a signal of a groundswell against the status quo among the intellectuals in the same way as "socialism" served as a groundswell for an earlier generation (p. 196). And yet he asks: Of what political utility is a deconstructive reading? And what politics are served by helping students set aside the metaphysical ideas presupposed by humanistic ways of reading the traditional literary canon? Rorty's blindspot, it seems, is precisely the Derridean political effects of a critique of humanism and of forms of liberalism insofar as they unproblematically reproduce or found themselves on one or another version of the humanist subject. Yet the story he has to tell about Derrida is right enough to be interesting, and we will return to this later on in this book.

Derrida's Political Pedagogy

Derrida's pedagogy is political in the sense that it teaches us to read and write *differently*. So we can expect to unpack the pedagogy by reference to a history of the concept of "difference." As such it is a pedagogy that calls into question the "hard core" metaphysical assumptions protecting the Western institutions of reading and writing, not just the written word but also extratextual practices of speaking and acting (insofar as they are historically tied to notions of freedom and still open to definition within international law).

Consider the way Rorty tells the story. Derrida follows the Nietzsche-Heidegger line of thought that repudiates Platonism as the source of all metaphysics in the West from St Paul to Kant, Mill, and Marx. Heidegger still sees in Nietzsche the last strands of an inverted Platonism, tied to the metaphysics of the *will to power*, and pictures himself as the first genuinely *post*-metaphysical thinker. Derrida, in his turn, acknowledges his debt to Heidegger and agrees with him that the most important philosophical task is to break free from the "logocentrism" based upon self-presence, immediacy, and univocity that together govern a set of inherited metaphysical dualisms and oppositions, clouding our view and manifesting nihilistic impulses in our culture. Even so, Derrida detects in Heidegger's notions of Being and the "ontological difference" a residual and nostalgic vestige of metaphysics.

Deconstruction for Derrida substitutes a critical practice focused upon texts for the ineffable or the inexpressible. It does so, not by trying to escape the metaphysical character of language but by exposing and undermining it. As a critical practice, then, it fixes upon the peripheral and accidental aspects of the textual system to subvert its main message, playing off rhetorical elements against grammatical structure. The term "deconstruction" denotes a particular kind of practice in reading and, thereby, a method of criticism and mode of analytical inquiry related to difference.

Barbara Johnson (1981) clarifies as follows:

> Deconstruction is not synonymous with "destruction," however. It is in fact much closer to the original meaning of the word "analysis" itself, which etymologically means "to undo"—a virtual synonym for "to de-construct."...If anything is destroyed in a deconstructive reading, it is not the text, but the claim to unequivocal domination of one mode of signifying over another. A deconstructive reading is a reading, which analyses the specificity of a text's critical difference from itself.

Of course, this applies not just to literary texts or the literary canon but to all texts and canons—an application accompanied by the thought that texts and discourses occupy a central place in the political, that politics has its own canon and set of texts that can be read deconstructively, that, perhaps, all that politics—at least, in terms of tradition and even in the face of the changing technologies shaping today's mass media—is a set of texts or text-analogues where the radical concordance of text, image, and sound are interwoven. This pedagogy, then, is a process that allows us to interrogate the institution of literature, of publishing and texting in relation to the subject and the citizen, and beyond that, to new forms of communication and media, and the concept of democracy itself.

The question of pedagogy is central for Derrida not only in terms of teaching us to read and write differently as a means of appreciating the complex relations of metaphysics and politics and how one grows out of the other—how politics often harbors deep metaphysical commitments that are never articulated or consciously realized. As a man, a philosopher, and a teacher, he was also very much dedicated to the processes of speech, teaching, and writing as the principal means of literature and the university in fulfilling their roles within a democracy.

Pedagogy and politics are thus central and interrelated aspects for Derrida—after all, he does talk explicitly about the role of intellectuals, the university, racism, and multiculturalism. This suggests a "pedagogy of difference" (see Trifonas, 2003) and registers the very clear sense in which deconstruction is relevant to both education and pedagogy (see Biesta & Egéa-Kuehne 2001; Trifonas & Peters, 2004). In the 1980s and 1990s, Derrida came to influence a range of radical educators, including Henry Giroux, Gregory Ulmer, Peter

Trifonas, Roger Simon, Denise Egéa-Kuehne, Patti Lather, Gayatri Chakravorty Spivak, Gert Biesta, Michael Peters and many others. His legacy in education and pedagogy will continue to grow as educators, teachers, and students continue to explore the complexity and fullness of his opus and its significance for politics and pedagogy.

The Promise of Politics and Pedagogy

In this book, we bring together six chapters and a postcript in which we continue our exploration of politics and pedagogy and their interconnections in Derrida's work. They are not meant as the final word on Derrida and education—if such a thing were possible in the first place. They are rather, in a more Rortyan register, part of an ongoing conversation with Derrida—not only about the significance of Derrida's work for our understanding of educational processes and practices, but also about ways in which we can think and do education differently "after" Derrida.

Chapter 1 immediately goes to the heart of Derrida's work by showing how deconstruction is driven by "justice" understood as a concern for the other. This already reveals the ethicopolitical horizon of Derrida's work and the affirmative character of deconstruction more generally. The concern for the other—or to be more precise, the concern for the unforeseeable incoming of the other, for the promise of the other—is the point where deconstruction and education connect. Chapter 2 continues the discussion of this theme by exploring Derrida's humanism—a humanism that is not "onto-theological" but explicitly political. The chapter not only argues that deconstruction is never neutral but always intervenes. It also discusses Derrida's particular intervention in the heritage of Enlightenment humanism. Chapter 3 looks in more detail at the question of the human subject in Derrida's work and argues, against Derrida's critics, that a new "understanding" of human subjectivity is at the center of Derrida's idea of a "democracy to come." Along these lines, the chapter shows the political nature of Derrida's humanism. Chapter 4 explores Derrida's connection to the critical tradition in modern philosophy by presenting deconstruction as a form of critical philosophy that offers an alternative to the two main critical "styles" of modern philosophy: critical dogmatism and transcendental critique. Derrida's "quasi transcendentalism" takes the question of critique away from truth and rationality and turns it towards justice, thus showing that the "point" of the critical work performed by deconstruction is inherently ethicopolitical and inherently educational. Chapter 5 raises the question of what might happen to (our understanding) of education "after" deconstruction. The chapter explores the humanist foundations of modern education and shows how Derrida's "inventionalism" provides a way for distinguishing between education and socialization that is not based upon a truth about the human being but is characterized by a concern for the event of the invention of the other. Chapter 6 returns to the question of the future of the humanities in the context of higher education and Derrida's idea of the university "without conditions." The chapter shows once more that education is not simply a field to which Derrida's ideas might be applied, but that the question of education is at the very heart of what we perhaps might best summarize as Derrida's "political humanism." Derrida's humanism is not a humanism that aims to specify what the human being is or ought to be. It rather is a humanism that is characterized by an openness towards the future, towards the incalculable, and the unforeseeable and, most importantly, towards the promise of the incoming of the other. As we show in the chapters that follow, this is at the very same time the question of politics and the question of pedagogy "after" deconstruction.

Notes

1. "Jacques Derrida in Memoriam" can be found at http://www.humanities.uci.edu/remembering_jd. The web page contains a selection of letters from Derrida's admirers among scholars such as Butler, Spivak, and Hollier, as well as additional statements.
2. See http://www.nationalreview.com/comment/miller_molesky200410130841.asp.
3. See http://www.flynnfiles.com/archives/culture2004/jacques_derrida_rip.html and http://www.twonotesolo.com/blogs/2004/10/future-perfect-pie-in-face.html, respectively.
4. Wittgenstein, strongly influenced by Freud in this regard, openly talked of philosophy as a disease (dis-ease) that could be cured only by doing more. He also suggested that his new way of doing philosophy (in the *Investigations*) was therapeutic. More precisely, we can talk perhaps about the way in which philosophy as an institution, like many other disciplines, policies its borders, disciplines its students, controls its members, prevents its intellectual crises in the shift of paradigms, treats its outcasts, and protects its "core."
5. Barry Smith (Editor, *The Monist*) instigated the letter. The signatories were: Hans Albert, David Armstrong, Ruth Barcan Marcus, Keith Campbell, Richard Glauser, Rudolf Haller, Massimo Mugnai, Kevin Mulligan, Lorenzo Pena, Willard van Orman Quine, Wolfgang Rod, Edmund Ruggaldier, Karl Schuhmann, Daniel Schulthess, Peter Simons, Rene Thom, Dallas Willard, and Jan Wolenski.
6. In this context, it is interesting to note that Ruth Barcan Marcus, the Halleck Professor of Philosophy at Yale, wrote to the French government (Ministry of Research and Technology) on March 12, 1984 to protest Derrida's nomination to the position of Director of

the International College of Philosophy, citing Foucault's alleged description of Derrida as practicing "*obscurantisme terroriste*." Derrida was teaching at Yale at the time. He remarks upon this affair in a footnote to "Afterword: Toward an Ethic of Discussion" in *Limited Inc*. (Derrida, 1988: 158–159) in relation to the exchange with John Searle, who used the same epithet as Marcus in an article published in the *New York Review of Books*. In relation to Searle's usage, Derrida remarks: "I just want to raise the question of what precisely a philosopher is doing when, in a newspaper with a large circulation, he finds himself compelled to cite private and unverifiable insults of another philosopher in order to authorize himself to insult in turn and to practice what in French is called a *jugement d'autorité*, that is, the method and preferred practice of all dogmatism" (p. 158). He comments upon the "Marcus affair" in the same footnote in the following terms: "I have cited these facts in order better to delimit certain concepts: in such cases, we are certainly confronted with chains of repressive practices and with the police in its basest form, on the border between alleged academic freedom, the press, and state power" (p. 159).
7. "Philosophy as a Kind of Writing" is the title of an essay by Richard Rorty that appears in his *Consequences of Pragmatism*, Brighton, Harvester Press, 1982: 90–109.
8. See his essay "The Time of the Thesis: Punctuations" (1983b), where he reflects upon his preoccupations of (at that point) the last twenty-five years of scholarship, beginning with his 1957 thesis "The Ideality of the Literary Object." The essay itself is a reflection upon the philosophical form of the "thesis."

References

Biesta, G. & Egéa-Kuehne, D. (2001) *Derrida & Education*. London, Routledge.
Derrida, J. (1983) "The Principle of Reason: The University in the Eyes of its Pupils," *Diacritics* 13.3: 3–20.
Derrida, J. (1984) "Languages and Institutions of Philosophy," *Semiotic Inquiry/Recherches Semiotiques* 4.2: 91–154.
Derrida, J. (1985) "Racism's Last Word," *Critical Inquiry* 12.1: 290–299.
Derrida, J. (1986a) "Declarations of Independence," *New Political Science* 15: 7–15.
Derrida, J. (1986b) "Literature and Politics," *New Political Science* 15 (Summer): 5.
Derrida, J. (1988) "Afterword: Toward an Ethic of Discussion," in Gerald Graff (ed.), Samuel Weber (trans.), *Limited Inc*. Evanston, IL: Northwestern University Press. pp. 111–154.
Derrida, J. (1989) "On Colleges and Philosophy," in Lisa Appignanesi (ed.), *Postmodernism: ICA Documents*. New York: Columbia University Press. pp. 66–71.
Derrida, J. (1990) "Force of Law: The Mystical Foundation of Authority," *Cardozo Law Review: Deconstruction and the Possibility of Justice* 11.5–6: 920–1045.
Derrida, J. (1992a) "Mochlos, or the Conflict of the Faculties," in Richard Rand (ed.), *Logomachia*. Lincoln: University of Nebraska Press. pp. 1–34.
Derrida, J. (1992b) "Interview with Jacques Derrida and Letter by Barry Smith," *Cambridge Review* (October): 131–139.
Derrida, J. (1992c) *The Other Heading: Reflections on Today's Europe*. Pascale-Anne Brault & Michael B. Naas (trans.). Bloomington: Indiana University Press.
Derrida, J. (1994) *Specters of Marx: The State of the Debt, the Work of Mourning, & the New International*. Peggy Kamuf (trans.). London: Routledge.

Derrida, J. (1995) "Is There a Philosophical Language?" in E. Weber (ed.), P. Kamuf & others (trans.), *Points... Interviews, 1974–1994*. Stanford, CA: Stanford University Press.
Derrida, J. (1997a) "The Politics of Friendship," *Journal of Philosophy* 75.11: 632–645.
Derrida, J. (1997b) *Politics of Friendship*. George Collins (trans.). London: Verso Books.
Derrida, J. (1998) *Monolingualism of the Other or the Prosthesis of Origin*. Stanford, CA: Stanford University Press.
Habermas, J. (1981) "Modernity vs Postmodernity," *New German Critique*, 22, Special Issue on Modernism (Winter, 1981): 3–14.
Habermas, J. (1987) *The Philosophical Discourse of Modernity: Twelve Lectures*. Frederick Lawrence (trans.). Cambridge, MA: The MIT Press.
Johnson, B. (1981) "Translator's Introduction," to J. Derrida, *Dissemination*. Chicago: Chicago University Press.
Nigro, R. (2005) "Derrida's Last Conference," *German Law Journal* 6.1 (January 1).
Peters, M. & Marshall, J. (1999) *Wittgenstein: Philosophy, Postmodernism, Pedagogy*. Westport, CT & London: Bergin & Garvey.
Rorty, R. (1991) "Is Derrida a Transcendental Philosopher?" in *Essays on Heidegger and Others: Philosophical Papers*, Vol. 2. Cambridge, UK: Cambridge University Press, pp. 119–128.
Rorty, R. (1998a) "Habermas, Derrida, and the Functions of Philosophy," *Truth and Progress: Philosophical Papers*. Cambridge: Cambridge University Press. pp. 307–326.
Rorty, R. (1998b) "Deconstruction," in Raman Selden (ed.), *From Formalism to Poststructuralism*, Vol. 8 of *The Cambridge History of Literary Criticism*. Cambridge: Cambridge University Press.
Trifonas, P. (2003) *Pedagogies of Difference: Rethinking Education for Social Change*. New York; London: RoutledgeFalmer.
Trifonas, P. & Peters, M.A. (eds.) (2004) *Deconstructing Derrida: Tasks for the New Humanities*. New York: Palgrave.

· 1 ·

DECONSTRUCTION, JUSTICE, AND THE VOCATION OF EDUCATION

GERT BIESTA

Deconstruction[1] has often been accused of being a form of critical analysis that aims at tearing apart everything it finds on its way. It has been characterized as a form of textualization with hyper-relativistic and nihilistic implications. Deconstruction, so the argument goes, is, therefore, ethically void, politically impotent, and utterly dangerous (see, e.g., Ferry & Renaut, 1990; Habermas, 1988; see also Fleming, 1996; Hoy, 1989). In this chapter, I wish to argue that such allegations seriously miss the point—or better points (Derrida, 1995)—of deconstruction. What I wish to make clear is that deconstruction is not a skeptical or relativistic position (it isn't even "a" position), but that it has a distinct ethicopolitical motivation or, as Richard Bernstein has so aptly put it, a distinct ethicopolitical *horizon* (see Bernstein, 1992).

In its shortest and most general formula, the ethicopolitical horizon of deconstruction can be described as a concern for the other. Rather than being destructive, negative, or "an enclosure in nothingness," deconstruction rather expresses "an openness towards the other" (Derrida, 1984: 124). For that reason deconstruction can best be characterized as *affirmative*. The deconstructive affirmation of the other is not straightforwardly positive. It is not merely an affirmation of what already exists and, for that reason, can be known and identified. Deconstruction is an affirmation of what is *wholly* other. It is an affirmation of what is unforeseeable from the present, of what is beyond the horizon of the same (cf. Caputo, 1997: 42; see also Gasché, 1994). It is an affirmation of an other that is always to come, as an event that "as event, exceeds calculation, rules, programs, anticipations and so forth" (Derrida, 1992a: 27). More, therefore, than simply an openness towards the other, deconstruction is an openness towards the unforeseeable incoming (*l'invention*; invention) of the other. As Caputo has suggested, deconstruction might, therefore, best be thought of as an "inventionalism" (Caputo, 1997: 42).

The road towards the other is not an easy road. Derrida might say that it is an impossible road, that is, if we understand impossibility with Derrida as that which cannot be foreseen as a possibility It is, therefore, the very "experience of the impossible" (Derrida, 1992a: 15) that makes the invention, the incoming of the other possible. An invention, Derrida argues, "has to declare itself to be the invention of that which did not appear to be possible; otherwise it only makes explicit a program of possibilities within the economy of the same" (Derrida, 1989: 60). For this reason we might say that deconstruction is "the relentless pursuit of *the* impossible, which means, of things whose possibility is sustained by their impossibility, of things which, instead of being wiped out by their impossibility, are actually nourished and fed by it" (Caputo, 1997: 32).

In this chapter, I wish to provide an account of the "logic" of deconstruction in such a way that its ethicopolitical horizon can come into view. I will first, by way of example, address the impossible task of writing about Derrida and doing justice to his writings. I will then give a more formal account of several deconstructive themes, focusing on the deconstruction of logocentrism, on the ubiquity of writing, and on difference and *différance*, so as to make clear how all this leads to deconstruction's concern for the other—a concern to which Derrida not only refers as "justice," but with respect to which he has even claimed that deconstruction *is* justice (Derrida, 1992a: 35). In the final section, I will argue that deconstruction should not be conceived as a theory or a philosophy that can or should subsequently be applied to education. Deconstruction rather provides a way to think again and afresh, more strictly and more radically, about the concern that has been central to the "project" of education at least since the Enlightenment—a concern for precisely the incoming of the other, the coming of the other into the world (see also Biesta, 2006).

Reading Derrida—Writing after Derrida

In more than one sense, writing about Derrida is an impossible task. There is first of all the sheer volume of Derrida's publications and the fact that his work is quite often complex and difficult to read. Derrida has written, with, against, and in/on the margins of the texts of major thinkers in the Western tradition—such as Plato, Aristotle, Kant, Rousseau, Hegel, Nietzsche, Husserl, Freud, and Heidegger—both explicitly and between the lines. His writing often breaks with the conventional, linear presentation of philosophical argument and contains multiple experiments with typography, punctuation, and pictorial form.

But the problem of writing about Derrida is not just a technical problem. It is not just the problem of finding a way to represent a corpus that can hardly be represented because of its scale. It is not just the problem of conveying the original meaning of an oeuvre that is complex and unconventional. For it is precisely the assumption that meaning can be grasped in its original moment, that meaning can be represented in the form of some proper, self-identical concept, that Derrida has been most determinedly out to challenge. This may help to understand why Derrida's writing is often unconventional and oblique. His writing is a "writing on writing" (Derrida, 1983: 45) that doesn't want to betray itself, that doesn't want to restore the kind of order it puts into question. At the very same time, however, it is precisely this that makes writing *about* Derrida into a Catch 22, because getting Derrida "right," that is, giving the final representation of the original meaning of his oeuvre, is at the very same time *not* getting him right.

Understanding and Misunderstanding

This Catch-22 is not simply the last word about Derrida and deconstruction. For we might argue that the very *im*possibility of getting Derrida right is precisely what opens up the possibility of writing about Derrida in the first place (see Bennington, 1993: 15; 38). At this stage we can at least imagine that if our writing were to be identical with Derrida's writing, it would be impossible to recognize it as writing about Derrida (it would count not even as writing about Derrida). In order to "re-present" Derrida's writing, in order to say the same thing as he says, in order to capture his writing in its singularity, we are, therefore, obliged to say something different.

Both among followers and critics of Derrida, there are those who have taken this to mean that deconstruction is a kind of "hermeneutics free-for-all" (Norris, 1987: 139), a joyous release from all the rules and constraints of interpretation and understanding. But this interpretation, which suggests that deconstruction is basically a *skeptical* position, overlooks a crucial "movement" in Derrida's writing.

It is true, that Derrida has challenged the common understanding of writing and reading as two oppositional activities, one actively producing, the other passively consuming. Derrida has pointed to a certain complicity between writing and reading, in that a text needs to be read in order to be or become a text. This implies that writing—and human communication in general—always entails a *risk*: the risk of misunderstanding. If this were all there is to say, it might be correct to conclude that Derrida simply wants to invert the opposition between understanding and misunderstanding, so that the latter would henceforth take priority over the former and would thereby become the rule or the law. But this interpretation overlooks the fact that Derrida has not questioned the possibility of understanding as such, but first and foremost the way in which we conceive of the *relationship* between understanding and misunderstanding.

This relationship is commonly understood as a binary opposition, an opposition of two, mutually exclusive options. The opposition implies a hierarchy, in that understanding is considered to be the normal situation and misunderstanding the aberration. Understanding thus defines what "real" or "successful" reading is, while misunderstanding is conceived as the distortion of this normal situation, a distortion that comes from the "outside." As soon as it is acknowledged, however, that misunderstanding is always possible (which is not the same as saying that it is always the case), we need to ask whether we can still hold that misunderstanding constitutes an accident, that it is a risk that befalls communication from the outside. According to Derrida, this is not the case. He has argued that misunderstanding is as much a part of language and communication and is as much on the "inside" as understanding is (Derrida, 1988: 15–17). It, therefore, has to be conceived as "a *general possibility inscribed in* the structure of positivity, of normality, of the 'standard'" (Derrida, 1988: 157; emphasis in original).

From this it follows that the idea of normal communication as successful understanding is not a fact but rather an "ethical and teleological determination" of what normal communication is (Derrida, 1988: 17). This in turn means that the purity of normal communication can be maintained only by an act of exclusion. This not only reveals that what one tries to keep outside of communication (viz., misunderstanding) inhabits the inside, but also, Derrida holds, that there would not even be an inside without that fact. We might say, therefore, that the term excluded by the binary divide (understanding versus misunderstanding) returns to sign the act of its own exclusion—and, even more importantly, that this apparent complicity is precisely what outlaws the legality of this exclusion in the first place (see Bennington, 1993: 217–218; see also Derrida, 1981a: 41–42).

This reveals that deconstruction is far from an attempt to make misunderstanding the rule or the law. Derrida only wants to make clear that the structural possibility of misunderstanding must be taken into account when describing so-called normality, and also "that this possibility can neither be *excluded nor opposed*" (Derrida, 1988: 157). The condition of possibility of communication can, therefore, be found neither in pure understanding or pure misunderstanding, nor in some higher unity of understanding and misunderstanding. What Derrida rather wants to bring into view is the ultimate *undecidability* of this opposition, an undecidability that cannot be traced back to some original, pure unity, but that itself is always already "at work." At this point, we encounter the entirely different logic of the "originarity of the secondary" (Bennington, 1993: 40), the logic of "the supplement" (Derrida, 1976: 269–316). The logic, in short, of *différance* (Derrida, 1982: 1–28; see also below).

Translation, the Responsible Response

Having said all this, we are now in a better position to grasp the role of misunderstanding—the need to say something different if we want to say the same—in our writing about Derrida. Derrida has made us first of all aware of the fact that we are not in a position to *choose* between (pure) understanding and (pure) misunderstanding because the former is always already contaminated by the latter. Misunderstanding is the essential and hence necessary risk of all understanding. There is only one way to evade this risk, which is *not* to engage in an act of reading or interpretation at all. While this might be the only way to be absolutely respectful of the singularity of Derrida's writing, it makes this singularity opaque, silent, unidentifiable, and unrecognizable at the very same time. Such a singular would then be a failure in its own terms. This means that for the singular to be possible as a singularity, it must take the risk of a "repetition in alterity" (Bennington, 1993: 86), the risk of misunderstanding, the risk of *translation*—"and for the notion of translation we would have to substitute a notion of *transformation*" (Derrida, 1981a: 20). Only this repetition in alterity opens up the possibility for the singular to be recognized in its irreducible singularity (see Gasché, 1994: 14–15).

Writing about Derrida, therefore, means translating Derrida—"and the question of deconstruction is also through and through *the* question of translation" (Derrida, 1991: 270). Translation is not the transmission or reproduction of an original meaning that preceded it, because the originality of the original comes into view only *after* it has been translated (which in turn means that the very sense of a pure original preceding translation is but an effect of translation; see Derrida, 1985). Translation, then, might best be understood as a *response*, a response to the singularity of the text (see Gasché, 1994: 227–250). For this response to be a genuine response, it has to be *singular* itself (a "response without norms"; Derrida & Ewald, 1995: 289), and not just a repetition of the text or a response preprogrammed by the text.

This implies, however, that a genuine response has all the allure of irresponsibility: it is singular, untranslatable, and never an unconditional affirmation. And yet, for a response to be genuine and responsive, it also has to be *responsible* in that it needs to do justice to the singularity of the text (not in the least because the survival of the text is dependent on this response). After all a text lives only if it lives *on*,

> and it lives *on* only if it is *at once* translatable *and* untranslatable. ... Totally translatable, it disappears as a text, as writing, as a body of language [*langue*]. Totally untranslatable, even within what is believed to be one language, it dies immediately. (Derrida, 1979: 102)

Writing about Derrida, therefore, means responding to Derrida for the very sake of doing justice to Derrida's writing. How might this be achieved? Let me begin again.

From Metaphysics to the Other

> Since we have already said everything, the reader must bear with us if we continue on a while. If we extend ourselves by force of play. If we then *write* a bit: on Plato, who already said in the *Phaedrus* that writing can only repeat (itself), that it "always signifies (*sēmainei*) the same" and that it is a "game" (*paidia*). (Derrida, 1981b: 65)

The Myth of the Origin

The theme that runs through Derrida's writing right from the beginning is the theme of the *origin*—or, to be more precise, the theme of the thought of the origin, the theme of the philosophy of the origin, the theme, in short, of *metaphysics*.

Derrida has argued that the history of Western philosophy is one continuous attempt to locate a fundamental ground, a fixed permanent center, an Archimedean point, that serves both as an absolute beginning and as a center from which everything originating from it can be mastered and controlled. An origin that "closes off the play which it opens up and makes possible" (Derrida, 1978: 279). Since Plato, this origin has always been defined in terms of *presence*. The origin is thought of as fully present to itself and as totally self-sufficient. It is identical to itself and in this respect it conforms to the logic of identity. The "determination of Being as *presence*," Derrida holds, is the "matrix" of the history of metaphysics (which coincides with the history of the West in general) (see Derrida, 1978: 279).

> It could be shown that all the names related to fundamentals, to principles, or to the center have always designated an invariable presence—*eidos, archē, telos, energeia, ousia* (essence, existence, substance, subject) *alētheia*, transcendentality, consciousness, God, man, and so forth. (Derrida, 1978: 279–280)

The "metaphysics of presence" (Derrida, 1978a: 281) includes more than just the determination of the meaning of Being as presence. The metaphysical gesture of Western philosophy includes a *hierarchical axiology* in which the origin is designated as pure, simple, normal, standard, self-sufficient, and self-identical, in order *then* to think in terms of derivation, complication, deterioration, accident, etcetera. This is "*the* metaphysical exigency," that which has been "the most constant, most profound and most potent" (Derrida, 1988: 93).

Derrida has aimed to put this metaphysical gesture into question, although he has not been the first one to do so. Nietzsche, Freud, and Heidegger have all in their own way exposed and criticized the metaphysical desire—the desire for fixed, self-present origins—of Western philosophy (see Derrida, 1978: 280). But there is a crucial difference between Nietzsche's "demolition" or Heidegger's "destruction" of metaphysics and the work Derrida has been engaged in. Nietzsche, Freud, Heidegger, and all the other "destructive discourses" wanted to make a total break from the metaphysical tradition. They wanted to end and to overcome metaphysics. For Derrida, however, such a rupture is not a real possibility.

> There is no sense in doing without the concepts of metaphysics in order to shake metaphysics. We ... can pronounce not a single destructive proposition which has not already had to slip into the form, the logic, and the implicit postulations of precisely what it seeks to contest. (Derrida, 1978: 280)

While Derrida has definitely wanted to "shake" metaphysics, he has argued that this cannot be done from some neutral and innocent place "outside" of metaphysics. What is more to the point, to put it simply, is to say that Derrida has wanted to shake metaphysics by showing that it is itself always already "shaking," by showing, in other words, the impossibility of any of its attempts to fix or immobilize being through the presentation of a self-sufficient, self-identical presence.

This implies, among other things, that deconstruction is not something that is applied to the texts of the metaphysical tradition from the outside. It is, therefore, "not a method and cannot be transformed into one" (Derrida, 1991: 273). Rather

> "deconstructions," which I prefer to use in its plural form ... is one of the possible names to designate, in short by metonymy, what occurs [*ce qui arrive*], or cannot manage to occur [*ce qui n'arrive pas à arriver*], namely a certain dislocation which in effect reiterates itself regularly—and everywhere where there is something rather than nothing. (Derrida & Ewald, 1995: 287–288)

To which we need to add that "all sentences of the type 'deconstruction is X' or 'deconstruction is not X' *a priori* miss the point, which is to say that they are at least false" (Derrida, 1991: 275).

What Derrida has attempted to show in his readings of the texts of the Western tradition is that any presentation of a self-sufficient, self-identical presence can be done only with the help of that which is excluded by this presence. He has attempted to show, in other words, that presence cannot present itself but needs the "help" of what is not present, of absence. This puts the non-present in a kind of double position. On the one hand the non-present is what is totally different from what is present. And yet the presence *upon which its definition depends* can itself be articulated only with the help of that which it is not.

The Presence of the Voice

One of the most pervasive ways in which the metaphysics of presence has been present in Western philosophy is in the form of the privileging of voice as the medium of meaning and the consequent dismissal of writing as derivative and inessential. This order is based upon a rather straightforward logic in which spoken words are seen as the symbols of mental experience, and written words as the symbols of spoken words. The priority of spoken language over written or silent language stems from the fact that when words are spoken the speaker and the listener are supposed to be simultaneously present to one another. Writing, on the other hand, is considered to be subversive in so far as it creates a spatial and temporal distance between the author and its audience.

Derrida has referred to the privilege of the voice over writing as *phonocentrism*. *Phonocentrism* is in a sense a necessity, in that it is a phenomenon that occurs not only in Western culture but also in other cultures (see Derrida, 1984: 115–116). What is, however, a "uniquely Western phenomenon" is the translation of phonocentrism into a metaphysical system that assigns the origin of truth to speech or *logos* (Derrida, 1976: 3). Derrida has discussed this specifically Western response to the "phonocentric necessity" under the name of *logocentrism* (see Derrida, 1983: 40).

The deconstruction of logocentrism occupies a central place in Derrida's earlier writings, where he raises the question of whether it is possible to articulate the presence of speech (or speech as presence) in such a way that it is self-sufficient, simple, and identical with and present to itself—in such a way, in short, that it is pure and uncontaminated by what it is not, namely writing.

"Plato's Pharmacy," a long section in *Dissemination*, takes up the question of the priority of speech over writing in the form of a close reading of Plato's dialogue the *Phaedrus* (see Derrida, 1981b: 61–171). Plato's text presents itself as an attempt to articulate the priority of speech over writing and to show the philosophical, moral, and political dangers of thinking to invert that priority. What Derrida's reading of the *Phaedrus* reveals, however, is precisely the failure of the text to achieve what it argues. Most obvious in this respect is, of course, the fact that Plato argues for the inferior character of writing by means of writing itself. This predicament, which repeats itself wherever philosophy refuses to acknowledge its own textual status and aspires to a pure contemplation of truth, is a common pattern in the history of Western thought, for which reason we might say that logocentrism is first of all "the desire *not to recognize* this order of necessity" (Norris, 1987: 127).

What Derrida reveals in his reading of the *Phaedrus*—although this is far from the only place in his work where the point is made—is the impossibility of articulating the opposition between speech and writing as a stable opposition in which speech is the pure and self-sufficient origin and writing its derivative: completely opposite and completely external to speech. What his "deconstructive reading" makes clear, in other words, is that the presence of speech (as origin) cannot be articulated without the "help" of that which is thought of and defined as totally different from speech, without the "help" of what is absent.

From what we have seen so far, it will be clear that this should not be understood as a plea for the inversion of the opposition between speech and writing. After all, such an inversion would only replace one origin (speech) for another (writing) but would leave the metaphysical order itself, the order of original presence versus derivative absence, in its place. What Derrida has attempted to bring into view is the ultimate *undecidability* of the oppositions that constitute and govern this order—an undecidability that, contrary to Hegelian dialectics, can never be resolved in a "third term" (see Derrida, 1981a: 43)— and thereby the ultimate *impossibility* of articulating anything whatsoever as a pure, uncontaminated, self-present origin.

The Ubiquity of Writing

And yet there is a sense in which Derrida has indeed argued that "language is first … writing" (Derrida, 1976: 37)—a sense that immediately follows from the impossibility to grasp a pure, uncontaminated, self-present origin. To understand why this is so, we need to follow Derrida in his exposure of logocentrism in the traditional (metaphysical) theory of meaning. According to this theory, meaning is a relation of identity between a word and an object. Stated in more technical terms, a *sign* is a word. The sign "cow" is made up of the sound "cow," the *signifier*, and the concept or meaning of "cow," the *signified*. (The actual animal is the *referent*.) The relation between the signifier and the signified is understood in terms of *representation*. The signifier re-presents the signified, or, to be more precise, the signifier re-presents the *presence* of the signified. This implies that the presence of the signified is the origin of and the warrant for the meaning of the signifier. However, in order to serve as origin and warrant, the signified itself has to be *un*signified and *un*represented. It has to be what Derrida has called a "transcendental signified." The fact that the traditional theory of meaning depends upon the existence of an unsignified or transcendental signified reveals its logocentric character. "I have identified logocentrism and the metaphysics of presence as the exigent, powerful, systematic, and irrepressible desire for such a signified" (Derrida, 1976: 49).

But although it is a powerful desire, a desire so powerful that it has been able to exert its influence on almost every corner of Western thought, it is, as Derrida has attempted to show again and again, a desire that gets stuck in its own presuppositions. In its most simple form, this is, for the transcendental signified to be articulated as a presence, as an origin, it needs to be signified. But if this is so, then it follows that "every signified is also in the position of a signifier" (Derrida, 1981a: 20), that—in short—"*the thing itself is a sign*" (Derrida, 1976: 49).

According to the phonocentric order, speech is a sign of an original presence (e. g., of a thought), and writing is the signification of speech. The derivative character of writing can, therefore, be expressed by saying that writing is "a sign of a sign." As soon as it is acknowledged that the original, the thing itself is a sign, it follows that even the first act of signification is not the signification of an original but of something that itself is already signified. It follows, in other words, that the first act of signification already operates in the field of the sign of a sign. It is in this sense that Derrida has claimed that "language is first … writing." We should immediately add, however, that this is not writing in the traditional, logocentric understanding of the word. Derrida has called this kind of writing "arche-writing" (Derrida, 1976: 56) and has referred to the "science" of this writing as "Grammatology" (Derrida, 1976).

Difference and Différance

Precisely at this point we encounter one of the most complex though intriguing dimensions of Derrida's writing. The problem, stated simply, is that as soon as it is acknowledged that there are no simple, unsignified, transcendental signifiers that fix and warrant the meaning of our words, that there are no originals to which our words can refer, we come to a position where even this acknowledgment itself seems to have become "floating." The metaphysical tradition had tried to deal with this problem by "forgetting" the textual status of its own writing, by assuming that it was possible to occupy a place outside of the order of writing. Derrida's writing occurs beyond this naïveté. But he also acknowledges that there cannot be a total rupture, because such a rupture would deprive us of the very means to criticize metaphysics. Which puts Derrida in the awkward position "of having to account for an error by means of tools derived from that very error" (Johnson, 1981: x).

Derrida has tackled this predicament with the help of a theory of signs and of language developed by Ferdinand de Saussure. Contrary to the idea that language is essentially a naming process, attaching words to things, de Saussure had argued that language is a system, or a structure, where any individual element is meaningless outside the confines of that structure. In language, he holds, there are only *differences*. But—and here the ideas of Saussure coincide with Derrida's deconstruction of the metaphysics of presence—these differences are not differences between positive terms, that is between terms that in and by themselves refer to objects or things outside of the system. In language, Saussure argues, there are only differences *without* positive terms.

But if this is so, if there are no positive terms (which is the same as saying that there are no transcendental signifieds), then it follows that we can no longer articulate the differential character of language itself by means of a positive term either. Difference without positive terms implies that this dimension must itself always remain unperceived for, strictly speaking, it is unconceptualizable. It is a difference that cannot be brought back into the order of the same and, through a signifier, given an identity. This means, then, that "the play of difference, which, as Saussure reminded us, is the condition for the possibility and functioning of every sign, is in itself a silent play" (Derrida, 1982: 5).

If, however, we wish to articulate that which does not let itself be articulated and yet is the condition for the possibility of all articulation—which we might want to do (and this is crucial) in order to prevent metaphysics from reentering the field—we must first of all acknowledge that there can never be a word or a concept to represent this silent play. We must also acknowledge that this play cannot simply be exposed, for "one can expose only that which at a certain moment can become *present*" (Derrida, 1982: 5). And we must finally acknowledge that there is nowhere to begin, "for what is put into question is precisely the quest for a rightful beginning, an absolute point of departure" (Derrida, 1982: 6). All this, and more, is acknowledged in the new "word" or "concept"—"which is neither a word nor a concept" (Derrida, 1982: 7) but a "neographism" (Derrida, 1982: 13)—of *différance*.[2]

The reason why Derrida has introduced that "what is written as *différance*" (Derrida, 1982: 11) is not difficult to grasp. For although "the play of difference" is identified as the condition for the possibility of all conceptuality, we should not make the mistake to think that we have finally found the real origin of conceptuality, that, in other words, this play is a playful but nonetheless transcendental signified. Strictly speaking there is only one way to avoid this mistake, which is by acknowledging that the differences that constitute the play of difference "are themselves *effects*" (Derrida, 1982: 11). As Derrida argues,

> What is written as *différance*, then, will be the playing movement that "produces"—by means of something that is not simply an activity—these differences, these effects of difference. This does not mean that the *différance* that produces differences is somehow before them, in a simple and unmodified—in-different—present. *Différance* is the non-full, non-simple, structured and differentiating origin of differences. Thus, the name "origin" no longer suits. (Derrida, 1982: 11)

This means that in the "most classical fashion," that is, in the language of metaphysics, we would have to speak of them as effects "without a cause" (Derrida, 1982: 12). This in turn means "*that différance is not*, does not exist, is not a present-being (*on*) in any form; ... it has neither existence nor essence"

(Derrida, 1982: 6). Most certainly *différance* is not differentiation, because that would leave open the possibility "of an organic, original, and homogeneous unity that eventually would come to be divided" (Derrida, 1976: 13).

Although *différance* is directly related to a structuralist conception of meaning—which Derrida acknowledges when he says that he sees no reason to question the truth of what Saussure says (Derrida, 1976: 39)—there is one crucial aspect in which *différance* is beyond structuralism. The point here is that Derrida explicitly denies the original character of structure itself. Structure is *not* a transcendental signified (for which reason Derrida adds that he does not want to question the truth of what Saussure says "*on the level on which he says it*" but does want to question the logocentric way in which Saussure says it; see Derrida, 1976). Structure is even less the effect of an original presence preceding and causing it (see Derrida, 1978: 278–279). What *différance* tries to articulate is the differential character of the "origin" of structure itself. It is in this sense that we might say that Derrida's writing is post-structural—although we should add that the word "post-structuralism" was unknown in France "until its 'return' from the United States" (see Derrida, 1991: 272).

Deconstruction and the Other

The preceding pages may have given the impression that deconstruction is a highly technical enterprise and that Derrida's writing has primarily been addressed to fellow philosophers. Although Derrida has acknowledged that the central question of his writing is the question "from what site or non-site (*non-lieu*) philosophy [can] as such appear to itself as other than itself, so that it can interrogate and reflect upon itself in an original manner [?] (Derrida, 1984: 108), this reflection of philosophy upon itself is not conducted for its own sake. Derrida's writing has, among other things, been aimed at dismantling our preconceived understanding of identity as self-sufficient presence, in order to expose us to the challenge of hitherto concealed, excluded, and suppressed otherness—an otherness that has been ignored in order to preserve the very illusion of identity as self-sufficient presence. Derrida's writing has aimed to reveal that the otherness that is excluded and suppressed in order to maintain the myth of a pure and uncontaminated original presence is actually constitutive of that which presents itself as pure, self-sufficient, and self-present and, therefore, as totally different from this otherness. What the deconstruction of logocentrism brings into view, therefore, is—to put it "in a nutshell" (Caputo, 1997)—that "identity *presupposes* alterity" (Derrida, 1984: 117).

Although we might say, with Derrida, that the deconstruction of logocentrism is a search for "the other of language" (Derrida, 1984: 123), this does not mean that deconstruction is primarily concerned with a linguistic problematic. The question of alterity is first and foremost the question of the concrete other, of "the other, which is beyond language" (Derrida, 1984: 123). Far, then, from being a philosophy that, according to its critics, declares that there is nothing beyond language and that we are imprisoned in language, deconstruction can be seen as a *response*. "Deconstruction is, in itself, a positive response to an alterity which necessarily calls, summons or motivates it. Deconstruction is, therefore, vocation—a response to a call" (Derrida, 1984: 118).

It is precisely on this issue that Derrida's writing demonstrates a strong affinity to the work of Emmanuel Levinas, whose work stands out as an unprecedented attempt in modern philosophy to articulate what it means to do justice to the other as what he or she is, namely other (on the relationship between Derrida and Levinas, see especially Critchley, 1999). Derrida has contended that he is prepared to agree with everything Levinas has said and that the differences between them are of a biographical and not of a philosophical nature (see Derrida, 1986: 74–75).

The central insight of Levinas's writing is that Western philosophy has been unable to recognize the alterity of the other because it understands the relationship between man and world (including other men) primarily as an *epistemological* relationship, a relationship where an isolated, self-present mind or ego attempts to get accurate knowledge of the external world. Levinas refers to this gesture of Western philosophy, in which the ego or subject is the origin of all knowledge and meaning, as *egology*. The main implication of the epistemological preoccupation of modern philosophy is that the other can appear only as an object of knowledge. Further, for something to be (or become) an object of knowledge, it has to be conceptualized, which means that it has to be identified as an instance of some more general concept. If, however, the other can be thought of only as the outcome of the ego's act of conceptualization, and if, as a result, the other can be thought of only as an instance of something more general, the other can never appear in its "radical alterity," the other can never appear as "absolutely other," as a unique and irreducible *singular* (see, e.g., Levinas 1979; see also Llewelyn, 1995).

For Levinas this means that if we want to recognize the other in its alterity, we must, in a sense, reverse the philosophical order and take the "encounter" with the other as our point of departure instead of any metaphysical determination of being. It is for this reason that Levinas has referred to ethics as "first philosophy" (although it will be clear that in the reversal "first philosophy" itself has changed its meaning). In his essay on Levinas (Derrida, 1978: 79–153), Derrida has argued that the Levinasian reversal implies that we cannot say and also that we do not have to wonder what this encounter with the absolutely other is.

> There is no way to conceptualize this encounter: it is made possible by the other, the unforeseeable "resistant to all categories." Concepts suppose an anticipation, a horizon within which alterity is amortized as soon as it is announced precisely because it has let itself be foreseen. The infinitely-other cannot be bound by a concept, cannot be thought on the basis of a horizon; for a horizon is always a horizon of the same, the elementary unity within which eruptions and surprises are always welcomed by understanding and recognized. (Derrida, 1978: 95)

It is for this reason that Derrida has argued, as we have seen, that the affirmative character of deconstruction is not merely *positive*, that is, not merely an affirmation of what already exists and known, but that it is an affirmation of what is *wholly* other (*tout autre*) (see Derrida, 1992a: 27).

Against this background, Derrida does raise the question, however, whether Levinas can consistently hold that the only way to do justice to the alterity of the other is by resisting any conceptualization. Derrida doubts whether this can be done so easily. "One could neither speak, nor have any sense of the totally other," he has argued, "if there was not a *phenomenon* of the totally other, or evidence of the totally other as such" (Derrida, 1978: 123). There seems to be, therefore, a certain necessity for a conceptualization of the other, a necessity to which Derrida refers as *transcendental violence* (Derrida, 1978: 118–133). It is violent because it *presents* the non-representable (the other as other). It is transcendental because this representation is the very condition of possibility of any recognition of the other as other other.[3]

Having arrived at this point—although the point of deconstruction lies more in the crossing than in the arrival—I wish to call to memory the "law of singularity," the law of the inevitable dissingularization of the singular through the repetition-in-alterity without which it could not hope to secure its singularity (Gasché, 1994: 14–15). After all, if there is a point in Derrida's writing, it resides in the recognition that the singularity of the other requires a "minimal universality" to be itself and to be recognized as such, and that without the risk involved—a risk that is both violent and necessary—no justice can possibly be done to the singularity of the other (see Gasché, 1994: 16).

Deconstruction, Justice, and the Vocation of Education

In the preceding pages, I have crossed deconstruction in two different ways. If something can be concluded from these crossings, it is that deconstruction cannot be presented as a position, and that in that sense it is not even "a" philosophy. Deconstruction has to be understood as an occurrence or event—or, to be even more precise, it has to be understood in its occurrence. What is at stake in the occurrence of deconstruction is an attempt to bring into view the impossibility to totalize, the impossibility to articulate a self-sufficient, self-present center from which everything can be mastered and controlled. Deconstruction reveals that every inside has a constitutive outside that is not merely external but in a sense always already inhabits the inside, so that self-sufficiency or self-presence can be brought about only by an act of exclusion. What gives deconstruction its motive and drive is precisely its concern for—or, to be more precise, its wish to do justice to—what is excluded.

The main problem of deconstruction, which has been the cause of many "misunderstandings" and "misinterpretations," lies in what I propose to call its *reflexivity*, that is, the fact that its conclusions (which are by no means endings) constantly subvert its assertions. How, for example, not to totalize the non-totalizable? How not to conceptualize the unconceptualizable. How not to speak? But rather than simply evading these aporias—which has been the common strategy of Western philosophy, placing itself outside of the scene of re-presentation—deconstruction faces these aporias heads on and tries to make its strength out of it.

We have already seen how this works out with respect to the deconstruction of metaphysics. Metaphysics, so we could say, was the traditional way in which philosophy (perhaps unconsciously) tried to evade the problem of reflexivity. Philosophy assumed that it had a special access to the ultimate ground(s) of existence. Derrida has revealed the impossibility of the metaphysical gesture. But rather than aiming at the construction of a *post*-metaphysical or anti-foundational philosophy, Derrida acknowledges that a total rupture with the metaphysical tradition of philosophy is impossible. We always already inhabit the "inside" of the metaphysical tradition. The main reason, however, for the deconstruction of metaphysics—or, to be more precise, for revealing the fact that metaphysics deconstructs itself (auto-deconstruction)—is not to come to terms with metaphysics as such. It is motivated by a concern that is explicitly ethical and political.

In a chapter in his *Deconstruction and the Possibility of Justice* (Derrida 1992a), Derrida wrote that ethical and political issues have not occupied a prominent place in most of his writings up to that point. He has acknowledged that "there are no doubt many reasons why the majority of texts hastily identified as 'deconstructionist' ... seem, I do say *seem*, not to foreground the theme of justice (as theme, precisely), or the theme of ethics and politics" (Derrida, 1992a: 7). Yet it was normal, foreseeable, and desirable that studies of a deconstructive style should culminate in this problematic, and even that deconstruction has done nothing but address this problematic, if only "obliquely," since "one cannot speak *directly* about justice, thematize or objectivize justice, say 'this is just' and even less 'I am just'" (Derrida, 1992a: 10). That is to say, one cannot do all this "without immediately betraying justice" (ibid.). Why is this so?

The clue to Derrida's answer lies in the contention that justice is always directed towards the other. Justice, Derrida has argued, is "the relation to the other." Saying, therefore, that something is just or that one is just is a betrayal of the very idea of justice to the extent to which it forecloses the possibility for the other to decide whether justice has indeed been rendered. If justice is a concern for the other as other, for the otherness of the other, for an otherness that, by definition, we can neither foresee nor totalize, if justice, in short, always addresses itself to the singularity of the other (Derrida, 1992a: 20), we are obliged—in the very name of justice—to keep the unforeseen possibility of the incoming of the other, the surprise of the "invention" of the other open (see Derrida, 1989). This means, however, that the very possibility of justice is sustained by its impossibility. Justice is, therefore, "an experience of the impossible," where—and this is crucial—the impossible is *not* that which is not possible, but that which cannot be foreseen as a possibility (Derrida, 1992a: 16).

The implications of this insight are not restricted to the determination of whether a situation or a person is just but extend to the very definition of justice itself. Here again we can say that it is for the very sake of justice as a concern for the otherness of the other that we can never decide once and (literally) for all what justice is. Justice is, therefore, not a principle or a criterion (as this would mean that we would know right now what justice is), nor an ideal (as this would mean that we would now be able to describe the future situation of justice), not even a regulative ideal (which would still imply a description of what justice is, although with the implication that the ideal is not expected to be ever present in some future). It belongs to the very structure of justice itself that it can never be present (and, therefore, never will be present). It is by necessity, as Derrida would say, a "justice to come," which means that it is *always* to come (Derrida, 1992a: 27).

The impossibility of justice is not to be understood as "a" deconstruction of justice. To understand why this is so, we need to observe Derrida's distinction between justice and the law (*droit, loi*). By "the law" Derrida means the positive structures that make up judicial systems in virtue of which actions are said to be legal, legitimate, or properly authorized. For Derrida, the law is "essentially deconstructible" because the law is constructed in the first place (see Derrida, 1992a: 14–15). But the fact that the law is essentially deconstructible "is not bad news. We may even see in this a stroke of luck for politics, for all historical progress" (Derrida, 1992a: 14), because it opens up the possibility to *improve* the law.

> [The] law as such can be deconstructed and has to be deconstructed. That is the condition of historicity, revolution, morals, ethics, and progress. But justice is not the law. Justice is what gives us the impulse, the drive, or the movement to improve the law, that is, to deconstruct the law. Without a call for justice we would not have any interest in deconstructing the law. (Derrida, 1997: 16)

This reveals that deconstruction is not aimed at the destruction of the law but at the improvement of the law in the name of that which cannot be named. As Caputo summarizes, deconstruction "keeps an inventionalist eye open for the other to which the law as law is 'blind'" (Caputo, 1997: 131). And it is in this sense that Derrida can argue that deconstruction *is* justice (Derrida, 1992a: 35).

The Aporia of Justice

The fact that justice is not a criterion or a principle means that it is not something that we can have knowledge about and that we need to only apply. Again we can say that the law is applicable. We can see that we act in agreement with norms, with the law. But to speak of justice is not a matter of knowledge, it is not a matter of application and calculation.

> Justice, if it has to do with the other ... is always incalculable. ... Once you relate to the other as the other, then something incalculable comes on the scene, something which cannot be reduced to the law or to the history of legal structures. This is what gives deconstruction its movement. (Derrida, 1997: 17–18)

The claim that justice is not a criterion, that it has no ground, so that at the basis of all our decisions lies a radical *undecidability* that cannot be closed off by our decisions but that "continues to inhabit the decision" (Derrida, 1996: 87), could be taken as the contention that in the end, and despite all that it claims, deconstruction *is* destructive and relativistic. But this, of course, holds only as long as we assume that ethics and politics can exist only on some firm ground.

Against such a foundationalist point of view, Derrida argues that ethics and politics *begin* only when this undecidability, which makes the decision at the very same time "necessary and impossible," is acknowledged. For Derrida, therefore, deconstruction is a "hyper-politicization" (Derrida, 1996: 85). This is an aporia—but "we must not hide it from ourselves" (Derrida, 1992b: 41).

> I will even venture to say that ethics, politics, and responsibility, *if there are any*, will only ever have begun with the experience and experiment of the aporia. When the path is clear and given, when a certain knowledge opens up the way in advance, the decision is already made, it might as well be said that there is none to make; irresponsibly, and in good conscience, one simply applies or implements a program. ... It makes of action the applied consequence, the simple application of a knowledge or know-how. It makes of ethics and politics a technology. No longer of the order of practical reason or decision, it begins to be irresponsible. (Derrida, 1992b: 41; 45)

Perhaps one never escapes the program. But in that case, "one must acknowledge this and stop talking with authority about moral or political responsibility" (Derrida, 1992b: 41). This means, therefore, that "the condition of possibility of this thing called responsibility is a certain *experience and experiment of the possibility of the impossible: the testing of the aporia* from which one may invent the only *possible invention, the impossible invention*" (Derrida, 1992b: 41).

Just Education?

If from here we finally move to the question of education, it is not, as I have already suggested in the beginning of this chapter, in order to apply deconstruction to education. Education is not something that is external to deconstruction, just as deconstruction is not something that comes to education from the outside. Although there are many different ways in which deconstruction can be shown to be "the case" in education (for an excellent account focusing on knowledge and pedagogy, see Ulmer 1985; see also the contributions in Biesta & Egéa-Kuehne, 2001), what I wish to highlight here is that if deconstruction is vocation, that is, "a response to a call" (Derrida, 1984: 118), it is for that reason at the very heart of the "experience" of education. If, to put it differently, the experience of education is the experience of the singularity of the other, of the other as a singular being, then we can say that education has its proper place in deconstruction, just as deconstruction has its proper place in education.

The relationship between deconstruction, justice, and education is, in other words, anything but accidental.

Derrida does not tell us, however, how we should respond to the call in order to be just or to render justice. Unlike a whole generation of educators and educational theorists, often of a critical bent, Derrida does not try to give an answer to the question of how we can emancipate or liberate.[4] He rather invites educators to return to the question itself, to the question of what it could mean to respond to the call, to respond responsibly to the otherness of the other—and to return to this age-old question *today*.

Today is, among other things, the day where we have lost our "metaphysical comfort" (Rorty). But although we can no longer rely upon the certainties of metaphysics—including the metaphysics of the human being (see Biesta, 2006)—Derrida has been eager to stress that this does not land us in anti-foundationalism, relativism, or a communitarism where the wisdom of the community is the highest wisdom. Although Derrida has been more than perceptive of history, situation, location, difference, etcetera, he has continued to reckon with the possibility of the impossible, that is, with the possibility of that which cannot be foreseen as a possibility but which lies—structurally— *beyond*. The impossible possibility, in short, of justice.

Given this, can education be just? Will education be just? Perhaps one way to appreciate what we might learn from and how we might respond to deconstruction is to approach this question from the point of view of "transcendental violence" that, in a sense, expresses the same idea as what I have referred to as the "law of singularity." We could argue that the only way to do justice to the other, the other whom we dare to educate, is by leaving the other completely alone. It is not difficult to see that this neglect (which wouldn't even count as a border-case of education) would make the other unidentifiable and unrecognizable. This would definitely block the invention of the other and would, therefore, be utterly unjust. For education not to be unjust, some form of recognition of the other as other is needed. But as we have already seen, any form of recognition, although necessary, is at the very same a mis-recognition and for that reason violent. This seems to be the aporia of any education that doesn't want to be unjust. It is, however, the aporia that education has to reckon with. Can this be done? How can this be done?

In a discussion about ethical decisions, Derrida has stressed that although ethical decisions are impossible, they can, for the very reason of their being ethical decisions, not wait. This "aporia of urgency" (Derrida, 1992a: 26) means that the instance of decision is a "madness" (ibid.). One *has* to decide, but a just decision is impossible. And yet, it is this very mad impossibility that makes justice possible. How can we give a place to this madness? Perhaps, as Edgoose (2001) has suggested, it is enough—or at least something—if we are attentive to the *hesitation* that inhabits our decisions. Justice could perhaps come from the "failure of fluency," that is, from "ethical hesitation."

Just education—if such a thing exists—has to be on the outlook for the impossible invention of the other. The other, according to Derrida, "is not the possible." The other is "precisely what is not invented" (Derrida, 1989: 59–60). This means that "deconstructive inventiveness can consist only in opening, in unclosing, destabilizing foreclosionary structures so as to allow for the passage toward the other" (ibid.). But one should not forget that one does not make the other come. One lets it come by *preparing* for its coming. Education, in short, must, therefore, prepare for the incalculable.

Notes

1. "I use this word for the sake of a rapid convenience, though it is a word I have never liked and one whose fortune has disagreeably surprised me" (Derrida, 1983: 44), although "as time passes, and when I see so many people trying to get rid of this word, I ask myself whether there is not perhaps something in it" (Derrida, 1996: 85).
2. In French the difference between "différence" and "différance" is inaudible, which implies that this neographism is itself already a subversion of phonocentrism.
3. There is much more at stake with respect to the possible difference between Derrida and Levinas that the scope of this chapter enables me to address. For more on Levinas and the question of subjectivity see Biesta, 1999; 2006; 2008. For the very question about the idea of a "post-deconstructive subjectivity" see especially Critchley, 1999a: 51–82.
4. See Biesta, 2005, for a deconstructive appraisal of the critical tradition in education.

References

Bennington, G. (1993) "Derridabase," in G. Bennington & J. Derrida, *Jacques Derrida*. Chicago & London: University of Chicago Press.
Bennington, G. & Derrida, J. (1993) *Jacques Derrida*. Chicago & London: University of Chicago Press.
Bernstein, R.J. (1992) *The New Constellation. The Ethical-Political Horizons of Modernity/Postmodernity*. Cambridge, MA: MIT Press.
Biesta, G.J.J. (1999) "Radical Intersubjectivity. Reflections on the 'Different' Foundation of Education," *Studies in Philosophy and Education* 18, 4: 203–220.
Biesta, G.J.J. (2005) "What Can Critical Pedagogy Learn from Postmodernism? Further Reflections on the Impossible Future of Critical Pedagogy," in Ilan Gur Ze'ev (ed.), *Critical Theory and Crit-

ical Pedagogy Today. Toward a New Critical Language in Education. Haifa: Studies in Education (University of Haifa). pp. 143–159.

Biesta, G.J.J. (2006) *Beyond Learning: Democratic Education for a Human Future*. Boulder, CO: Paradigm Publishers.

Biesta, G.J.J. (2008) "Pedagogy with Empty Hands: Levinas, Education and the Question of Being Human," in D. Egéa-Kuehne (ed.), *Levinas and Education: At the Intersection of Faith and Reason*. London/New York: Routledge. pp. 198–210.

Biesta, G.J.J. & Egéa-Kuehne, D. (eds.) (2001). *Derrida & Education*. London/New York: Routledge.

Caputo, J.D. (ed.) (1997) *Deconstruction in a Nutshell. A Conversation with Jacques Derrida*. New York: Fordham University Press.

Critchley, S. (1999) *Ethics, Politics, Subjectivity*. London/New York: Verso.

Derrida, J. (1976) *Of Grammatology*. Baltimore & London: Johns Hopkins University Press.

Derrida, J. (1978) *Writing and Difference*. Chicago: University of Chicago Press.

Derrida, J. (1979) "Living On: Border Lines," in H. Bloom, P. De Man, J. Derrida, G.J. Hartman & J. Hillis Miller, *Deconstruction and Criticism*. New York: Seabury Press.

Derrida, J. (1981a) *Positions*. Chicago: University of Chicago Press.

Derrida, J. (1981b) *Dissemination*. Chicago: University of Chicago Press.

Derrida, J. (1982) *Margins of Philosophy*. Chicago: University of Chicago Press.

Derrida, J. (1983) "The Time of the Thesis: Punctuations," in A. Montefiore (ed.), *Philosophy in France Today*. Cambridge: Cambridge University Press.

Derrida, J. (1984) "Deconstruction and the Other. An Interview with Jacques Derrida," in R. Kearney (ed.), *Dialogues with Contemporary Continental Thinkers*. Manchester, UK: Manchester University Press.

Derrida, J. (1985) "Des Tours de Babel," in J.F. Graham (ed.), *Difference in Translation*. Ithaca: Cornell University Press.

Derrida, J. (1986) *Altérités*. Paris: Osiris.

Derrida, J. (1988) *Limited Inc*. Evanston, IL: Northwestern University Press.

Derrida, J. (1989) "Psyche: Inventions of the Other," in L.L. & W. Godzich (eds.), *Reading de Man Reading*. Minneapolis: University of Minnesota Press.

Derrida, J. (1991) "Letter to a Japanese Friend," in Kamuf (ed.), *A Derrida Reader: Between the Blinds*. New York: Columbia University Press.

Derrida, J. (1992a) "Force of Law: The 'Mystical Foundation of Authority,'" in D. Cornell, M. Rosenfeld & D.G. Carlson (eds.), *Deconstruction and the Possibility of Justice*. New York & London: Routledge.

Derrida, J. (1992b) *The Other Heading. Reflections on Today's Europe*. Bloomington, IN: Indiana University Press.

Derrida, J. (1995) *Points... Interviews, 1997–1994*. Stanford, CA: Stanford University Press.

Derrida, J. (1996) "Remarks on Deconstruction and Pragmatism," in Ch. Mouffe (ed.), *Deconstruction and Pragmatism*. London & New York: Routledge.

Derrida, J. (1997) "The Villanova Roundtable: A Conversation with Jacques Derrida," in J.D. Caputo (ed.), *Deconstruction in a Nutshell. A Conversation with Jacques Derrida*. New York: Fordham University Press.

Derrida, J. (1999) *The Ethics of Deconstruction: Derrida and Levinas. Expanded Second Edition*. Edinburgh: Edinburgh University Press.

Derrida, J. & Ewald, F. (1995) "A Certain 'Madness' Must Watch over Thinking. An Interview with Jacques Derrida," *Educational Theory* 45, 3: 273–291.

Edgoose, J. (2001) "Just Decide! Derrida and the Ethical Aporias of Education," in G.J.J. Biesta & D. Egéa-Kuehne (eds.), *Derrida & Education*. London/New York: Routledge. pp. 119–133.

Ferry, L. & Renaut, A. (1990) *French Philosophy of the Sixties. An Essay on Antihumanism*. Amherst: University of Massachusetts Press.

Fleming, M. (1996) "Working in the Philosophical Discourse of Modernity," *Philosophy Today* 40, 1: 169–178.

Gasché, R. (1994) *Inventions of Difference. On Jacques Derrida*. Cambridge, MA: Harvard University Press.

Habermas, J. (1988) *Der Philosophische Diskurs der Moderne*. Frankfurt am Main: Suhrkamp Taschenbuch.

Hoy, D.C. (1989) "Splitting the Difference: Habermas's Critique of Derrida," *Praxis International* 8: 447–464.

Johnson, B. (1981) "Translator's Introduction," in J. Derrida (ed.), *Dissemination*. Chicago: Chicago University Press.

Levinas, E. (1979) *Totality and Infinity*. Pittsburgh: Duquesne University Press.

Llewelyn, J. (1995) *Emmanuel Levinas. The Genealogy of Ethics*. London/New York: Routledge.

Norris, C. (1987) *Derrida*. Cambridge, MA: Harvard University Press.

Ulmer, G. (1985) *Applied Grammatology. Post(e)-Pedagogy from Jacques Derrida to Joseph Buys*. Baltimore & London: Johns Hopkins University Press.

· 2 ·

DERRIDA AS A PROFOUND HUMANIST

MICHAEL A. PETERS

Derrida, Politics, and Humanism

I met Jacques Derrida on only one occasion towards the end of his career, indeed, only a few years before his untimely death at the age of 74 in 2004. He had been invited to the University of Auckland, New Zealand, in August 1999 to give a public lecture "Forgiving the Unforgivable" and to participate in a conference and an edited collection dedicated to his work under the title *Derrida Downunder* (Simons & Worth, 2001). It was a surprise to everyone, including the organizers of *Derrida Downunder*, that the public lecture by Derrida filled the Auckland Town Hall to capacity, perhaps up to 2,000 people. This was truly an intellectual event for Auckland and New Zealand. I can't imagine any philosopher who would have demanded such an audience in a small country. The lecture "Forgiving the Unforgivable" was one that Derrida had given at a number of universities—at Natal and Western Cape in 1998, at Stanford, Monash, and Sydney in 1999—and his meditations on forgiveness appeared later in *On Cosmopolitanism and Forgiveness* (Derrida, 2002b) and as "To Forgive: The Unforgivable and the Imprescriptible" in *Questioning God* (Caputo et al., 2001).

I listened intently to his patient and careful unraveling of several texts and themes as he teased out meanings and created new associations and allusions as only Derrida can do. His presence was so palpable. Indeed he was, without doubt, the intellectual who has great presence, who kept me and most of the audience spellbound for the entire two and a half hours as he elaborated the labyrinthine textual structure in a creative reading that somehow transcended itself and demonstrated the epitome of reading as textual commentary. I was lucky enough to be invited to sit with him on a panel on the university along with three or four others and to address some questions to him about the "unconditional university"—a paper that he allowed me to include later in a collection edited with Peter Trifonas entitled *Deconstructing Derrida: Tasks for the New Humanities* (Trifonas & Peters, 2004). I also had the opportunity of presenting to him—and a diverse academic audience that bought together philosophers, literary theorist, Maori and postcolonial thinkers, sociologists, and others—a paper on Derrida as a political thinker. It is always difficult when you are discussing a thinker of Derrida's status while he is in the room. He came up to me immediately afterwards and was most gracious and accepting of what I had written about him. I had said that I regarded him as the very example of a political philosopher beginning:

> someone who systematically disassembled the biases and assumptions of an unashamed ethnocentrism deeply embraced by Western thinking and represented in his destabilization of logocentrism. I should have added that Derrida as a political philosopher was also strongly committed to the principles and fruits of the European Enlightenment and believed that it had within its traditions the intellectual resources that enable it to progressively address and overcome its shortcomings.

I went on to discuss Derrida's relation to neoliberalism by focusing on a range of his later political works and to analyze Derrida's notion of "democracy to come" (Peters, 2001). It is clear that Derrida has a particular relationship to Marx that continues his humanism while opening it to deconstruction. It is an early relationship sustained over time. In an interview with Jean-Louis Houdebine and Guy Scarpetta in 1972, Derrida (1981: 60) is asked to sketch the relationship of his economy of *writing* to the economy of a dialectical materialist logic, especially as regards "matter." Derrida responds by suggesting that in so far as his work can be described under the rubric of the "critique of idealism," it is at least in sympathy with Marxism but the theoretical elaboration between the two economies is *still to come* (p. 62). He argues that Marx's texts (and those of the rest of the canon of Marxism) should not be regarded as "finished elaborations" that are simply to be applied:

> These texts are not to be read according to a hermeneutical or exegetical method which would seek out a finished signified beneath a textual surface. Reading is transformational... But this transformation cannot be executed however ones wishes. It requires protocols of reading. (Derrida, 1981: 63)

Yet, for Marx's texts, Derrida responds: "I have not yet found any that satisfy me" (ibid.). Derrida discusses the concept of matter in relation to his reading of general economy based on a reading of Bataille ("From Restricted to General Economy: A Hegelianism without Reserve" in *Writing and Difference*) and he indicates that to the extent that matter in this economy designates radical alterity, "what I write can be considered 'materialist'" (p. 64). Later, Derrida explains how he would want to positively deconstruct the oppositions that help characterize "matter" and "materiality," given the way it is sustained through its oppositions to "spirit," "form," and "ideality."[1] There is a postponement in Derrida's early writings in his engagement with Marx and a search for the correct protocols for reading him. What he says of Hegel applies also to Marx: "We will never be finished with the reading or the rereading of Hegel" (p. 77).

Over two decades later, Derrida again returns to Marx in a lecture given in 1993 in two sessions at the University of California, Riverside, at an international colloquium organized under the title of "Whither Marxism?" by Bernd Magnus and Stephen Cullenberg. That lecture, augmented and clarified, became *Specters of Marx* (Derrida, 1994). In response to the question, Derrida responds:

> It will always be a fault not to read and reread and discuss Marx...and to go beyond scholarly "reading" or "discussion." It will be more and more a fault, a failing of theoretical, philosophical, political responsibility. When the dogma machine and the "Marxist" ideological apparatuses...are in the process of disappearing, we no longer have any excuse, only alibis, for turning away from this responsibility. There will be no future without this. Not without Marx, no future without Marx, without the memory and the inheritance of Marx: in any case of a certain Marx, of his genius, of at least one of his spirits. For this will be out hypothesis or rather our bias: there is more than one of them, there must be more than one of them. (Derrida, 1994: 13)

The outline of his answer is prefigured in his earlier sketchy remarks and in the new practices of reading.

Later the same year, I was lucky enough to be invited to a conference by Barry Hindess entitled "The End of Postmodernism?" held at the Australian National University to host the American neo-pragmatist Richard Rorty. Seated next to him at dinner, I made a remark to him favorably comparing the impact of his work with that of Derrida's. He responded in his characteristically deflationary style denying the comparison: "Derrida is a grand intellectual in the tradition of Zola and Sartre... The French demand someone of his stature every generation" (or words to that effect). Rorty was right: a visit by himself would not have resulted in the same massive turnout in New Zealand (and indeed Rorty had visited Auckland on at least two occasions). I am pressed to think of another contemporary philosopher who might have generated the same public attendance in New Zealand. Popper or Bertrand Russell in their day might have; Quine most certainly would not have, nor Davidson or Putnam. Although Foucault, had he ever visited New Zealand, probably would have drawn a similar crowd. In the age of Saatchi and Saatchi, where marketing has taken over the notion of the *concept* from philosophy (as Deleuze notes), the attraction of a mass audience to listen to a French philosopher seemed remarkable, especially in New Zealand where the intellectual culture is small and fragile and where difference is not easily tolerated.

Perhaps, one reason why Derrida generated so much public interest is because his work, for a philosopher, is enormously wide-ranging. It also speaks many languages and registers to many different audiences and is controversial by nature because he focuses on those questions that all human beings have a stake in. His enormous corpus of work spills over the disciplinary boundaries of the entire spectrum of the arts, humanities, and social sciences, from literary criticism and philosophy to architecture, cultural studies, and theology. He was also a provocateur, though decidedly less cocky and abrasive in his advancing years, I'm told.

Forgiving Derrida

Jacques Derrida, a Frenchman of Jewish extraction who was born and grew up in Algeria, is undoubtedly one of the world's most distinguished contemporary philosophers. As the Stanford University website (http://prelectur. stanford.edu/lecturers/derrida/) indicates, his work has been the subject in whole or part of some 400 books and "In the areas of philosophy and literary criticism alone, Derrida has been cited more than 14,000 times in journal articles over the past 17 years." This proves that his work is well cited though not necessarily universally acclaimed or appreciated. His work has been fiercely attacked by both conservatives and members of the radical left. The former deny he is a philosopher and the latter dismiss his work as frivolous and apolitical.

In the Introduction I described the infamous occasion in 1992 when twenty analytic philosophers attempted to intervene in the internal affairs of Cambridge University by protesting at the prospect of an honorary degree for Derrida. This is kind of oppositional activity was unheard of in the annals of Cambridge and one that soured relations between philosophers who practice a different kind of philosophy and their analytic Anglo-American counterparts. These philosophers in an imperious act attacked Derrida's style of philosophy charging that he had stretched academic scholarship beyond recognition and that Derrida's work was mainly received in fields outside philosophy. The attack indicated how destabilizing Derrida's style and work is for analytic philosophy. Strangely, the artifice of analytic philosophy had been disassembled at the hands on one of the signatories Quine who in the 1951 paper 'Two Dogmas of Empiricism' attacked two central underlying tenants of logical empiricism: the distinction between analytic and synthetic truths, and logical reductionism. After Quine's attack against analyticity it was no longer clear what philosophical analysis or analytic philosophy was. The interference was unprincipled, a transparent political act which even in terms of its own arguments failed miserably.

How does one represent Derrida and his writing? The linguistic notion of representation is central to Derrida's work and to his critique of Western metaphysics. He is suspicious of the view that language represents the world, at least in any straightforward sense. But "representation" is also important to him as a political principle indicating the ethical and political stakes in presenting an argument or representing a people, a text, an image, or (one's relation to) another thinker—the so-called politics of representation. Not least, the word "representation" captures his concerns for the genres of autobiography and confession, of philosophy as a certain kind of writing, of the "personal voice," and of the signature. Derrida is also careful of journalists and tends to refuse most invitations for interviews, especially by the popular press. Paradoxically, *Points... Interviews, 1974–1994* (Stanford University Press, 1995b), a collection, consisting of twenty-three interviews given over the course of the last two decades, provides a good introduction to Derrida (see especially his "The Work of Intellectuals and the Press").

Perhaps, more than any philosopher before him, and from his earliest beginnings, as I explain in the Introduction, Jacques Derrida has called attention to the form of "philosophical discourse"—its "modes of composition, its rhetoric, its metaphors, its language, its fictions," as he says—not in order to assimilate philosophy to literature but rather to recognize the complex links between the two and to investigate the ways in which the institutional authority of academic philosophy and the autonomy it claims rest upon a "disavowal with relation to its own language." (His doctoral thesis based on an investigation of Joyce purportedly investigated "The Ideality of the Literary Object", Derrida, 1983) The question of philosophical styles, he maintains, is itself a philosophical question.

"Deconstruction," the term most famously associated with Derrida, is a practice of reading and writing, a mode of analysis and criticism that depends deeply upon an interpretation of the question of style. In this, Derrida follows a Nietzschean-Heideggerian line of thought that repudiates Platonism as the source of all metaphysics in the West from St Paul to Kant, Mill, and Marx. Where Heidegger still sees in Nietzsche the last strands of an inverted Platonism, tied to the metaphysics of the will to power, and pictures himself as the first genuinely post-metaphysical thinker, Derrida, in his turn, while acknowledging his debt, detects in Heidegger's notion of Being a residual and nostalgic vestige of metaphysics. He agrees with Heidegger that the most important philosophical task is to break free from the "logocentrism" of Western philosophy—the self-presence, immediacy, and univocity—that clouds our view and manifests its nihilistic impulses in Western culture. And yet "breaking free" does not mean overcoming metaphysics. Deconstruction substitutes a critical practice focused upon texts on the ineffable or the inexpressible. It does so, not by trying to escape the metaphysical character of language but by exposing and undermining it: by fixing upon accidental features of the text to subvert its essential message and by playing off its rhetorical elements against its grammatical structure. Heidegger's strategy for getting beyond "man" will not do the trick: Derrida suggests that "a change of style" is needed, one that will "speak several languages and produce several texts at once," as he says in his earlier essay "The Ends of Man" (Derrida, 1982).

His Auckland lecture, "Forgiving the Unforgivable," (see Derrida, 2001) was an exemplary and unforgettable live performance of deconstruction, mapping the line between the conditional and unconditional use of "forgiveness," its limits and possibilities, its conceptual history in Judeo-Christian ethics, and its contemporary juridical and political contexts, focusing upon the "radical evil" of the Nazi death-camps. He began with the simple repetition of a single word—pardon—shorn of all context; he ended with the same repetition, but, having traversed its semantic space, he concluded with the performative (the speech-act) "pardon," as in "I beg your pardon (for keeping you so long)," "pardon," "thank you," "merci." He started with a series of preliminaries of what "forgiveness" is or might mean, noting the globalization of the use of "apology" in the political space with the Truth and Reconciliation Commission in South Africa, Bill Clinton's public apologies for Monicagate and for American (CIA) politics in South America, and the deliberate withholding of an apology for the bombing of Hiroshima and Nagasaki. He traced the genealogies of the lexical family of "forgiveness," "apology," and "pardon," sensitizing the audience to the pragmatics of context. He explored the Latin origin of "pardon," its meanings and usages in French, English, and German, and the way they carry over aporias of "the gift," "giving," "forgiving," "forgiveness" (*donner, le don, pardon*). With great seriousness and understanding, he played off their ambiguities and multiple meanings, exploring their meanings in various texts and their valencies in contemporary contexts: the Holocaust, decolonization, ethnic conflict, crimes against humanity. While he refrained from any direct comment, there were, of course, many resonances to the political and juridical contexts of "forgiveness" in New Zealand/Aotearoa between Maori and the Government. As he suggested, "forgiveness is an impossible truth or an impossible gift," and as he pondered, "Can one only forgive when speaking or sharing the language of the Other?"

Le Monde des Débats posed the question this way: "The pardon and repent have been the center of Jacques Derrida's seminar at the École des hautes études en sciences sociales for three years. What is the concept of the pardon? Where does it come from? Can it be imposed on everyone and all cultures? Does it have a place in the juridical order? The political? And under what conditions? But who grants it? And to whom? And in the name of what, of whom?" And Derrida responded to the question of pardon as follows:

> In principle, there is no limit to the pardon, no measure, no moderation, no "how much." On the condition, understood, of some "proper" sense of the word. What does one call "pardon"? What is it that calls for a "pardon"? Who calls, who calls something a pardon? It is as difficult to measure a pardon as to take the measure of such questions. For more reasons than I can be pressed to relate.
>
> 1. In the first place, because one maintains the equivocal, notably in political debate which reactivates and displaces today this notion—across the world they

maintain the equivocal. They often confound, sometimes in a calculated way, the pardon with related themes: excuse, regret, amnesty, prescription, etc., so many significations which certain people raise to law, to a penal law for which the pardon must remain in principle heterogeneous and irreducible.

2. If the concept of pardon remains enigmatic, it is because the scene, the figure, the language that they attempt to adjust belongs to a religious heritage (I say "abrahamique," to refer together to Judaism, the various Christianities and Islams). This tradition—complex and differentiated, even conflicting—is at once singular and on the way to universalization, across that which puts to work or brings to light a certain theatre of the pardon.

3. From there—and this is one of the threads of my seminar on the pardon (and perjury [parjure])—the very dimension of the pardon tends to be effaced in the course of this globalization, and with it all measure, all conceptual limit. In all the scenes of repenting, of plea, of pardon or excuse which have multiplied on the geopolitical scene since the last war, and in an accelerated way for some years, we see not only some individuals but entire communities, professional corporations, church representatives and hierarchs, sovereigns and chiefs of state asking for "pardon." http://fixion.sytes.net/pardonEng.htm

Derrida was a teacher par excellence. Christian Delacampagne (2006) shares an early statement made by Derrida in 1969 that foreshadowed Derrida's "le droit à la philosophie"—*the right to philosophize*, a right that he wanted to give to absolutely everybody, inside or outside academia (see his main texts on this subject in Jacques Derrida, *Du Droit à la philosophie* [Paris: Galilée, 1990]), suggesting that "Derrida's interest in questions of pedagogy started early in his professional career; and second, that his teaching was definitely politicized even in his formative years"

PHILOSOPHIE

Je propose d'organiser, à partir de l'année prochaine (1969–1970), avec la collaboration de tous les philosophes de l'Ecole (1) intéressés par un tel projet, un séminaire consacré à une

THEORIE DU DISCOURS PHILOSOPHIQUE

Dans un premier temps (l'année prochaine), les recherches pourraient se rapporter à certains problèmes concernant la langue philosophique (structure du signifiant philosophique ; histoire de la langue ; étymologie ; syntaxe. Signification et vérité. Rhétorique et philosophie : la rhétorique de la philosophie et la philosophie de la rhétorique ; langue naturelle, langue formelle et langue philosophique ; langage ordinaire et discours philosophique ; les ordres du signifiant [philosophique, scientifique, littéraire, poétique], etc.). Le fil conducteur pour ce premier trajet pourrait être:

Le statut de la METAPHORE dans le texte philosophique

Après une élaboration générale et préliminaire de la problématique (2), une série d'études spécialisées pourraient être coordonnées en fonction des travaux en cours à l'Ecole (maîtrise, thèse de troisième cycle, etc.). Il serait souhaitable, réciproquement, que l'orientation de certaines recherches à venir se tienne en rapport avec l'existence de ce séminaire. Il revient à tous les participants d'établir et de préciser les programme, contenu, méthode, procédure d'un tel séminaire. La première séance aura lieu le mardi 4 novembre à 16h30 en Salle des Résistants. Mais avant et après cette date je serai heureux de recevoir toutes les suggestions, propositions ou contre-propositions qu'on jugera utiles.

1. Il va de soi que ce séminaire sera aussi ouvert à tout non-philosophe et à tout chercheur étranger à l'Ecole qui sera en mesure d'y apporter une contribution positive.
2. Cette première phase pourrait être guidée par des questions de ce type : dans quelle mesure la généalogie philosophique des concepts qui peuvent nous servir à une telle élaboration, qu'ils soient issus directement de discours philosophiques de types divers ou qu'ils appartiennent à la rhétorique, à la linguistique, à la psychanalyse, etc. peut-elle limiter une telle théorie de la métaphore ? Dans quelle mesure la philosophie peut-elle s'assurer une domination pertinente de sa propre métaphorique, etc. ?

His seminars were legendry and demonstrate the care with which he prepared for these sessions. As the University of California at Irvine Critical Theory Archive (http://www.hydra.umn.edu/derrida/uci.html) notes, his seminar "was almost always fully written out (in either manuscript or typescript) and is supplemented with a variety of notes and photocopies." The Archive series documents almost every seminar that Derrida ever gave beginning in 1959 through to 1995, over 100 in total ranging over philosophers and the philosophical tradition in the early years—Malebranche, Ricoeur, Hume, Kant, Spinoza, philosophy of history, Husserl, Bergson, Heidegger—to his justly famous year-long seminars in the latter part of his career on "responding to the secret," "eating the Other," "the politics of friendship," "the right of philosophy," Paul de Man, hospitality, the death penalty, the pardon, justice. As the Archive notes "Typically, Derrida has taught at the Ecole normale supérieur (ENS) and at EHESS [L'Ecole des hautes Etudes en Sciences sociales] in winter, at Yale University and at Johns Hopkins University in the fall, and at the UCI in the spring."

The Relevance of Derrida: Against the New Moralists

The subtext of this book and the reading of Derrida as a "profound humanist" serve as a warning against the new moralizers—be they fundamentalist of any persuasion (Christian, Muslim, or Jewish), old unreformed classical liberal humanists, new humanists, secular or Christian—still searching for a theory of human nature on which to hang their sermons, or simply against those neoconservative humanists who, having rallied against an amorphous and unnamed nihilistic "postmodernism," falsely attribute the doctrine to Nietzsche or to his heirs. The new moralizers constitute a revival of an exclusive humanism demonstrating all the political and spiritual dangers of a set of essentialist beliefs in human nature—a theory or spiritual account—from which is derived who and what "we" are, the moral code "we" should follow, and both who belongs to the "we" and how those who belong should treat nonbelievers. In the USA, UK, and elsewhere, the term "the new moralizers" has been consistently applied to the social conservatives who have brought a new vision of morality based on a view of human nature and made it central to public policy, making determinations of individual virtue fundamental to welfare entitlement (Super, 2004). This shift in public policy paradigm has also been accompanied by the growth of conservative politics that has drawn upon the politicization of fundamentalist Christian groups going back to Ronald Reagan's administration.

The term fundamentalism itself originates in the late nineteenth century as a movement by evangelic Christians, against modernism, to affirm a set of "fundamental" beliefs, namely, "the five fundamentals"—the inspiration of the Bible by the Holy Spirit, the virgin birth, the belief that Christ's death was an atonement for sin, the bodily resurrection, and the historical reality of Christ's miracles. The new fundamentalism in American politics began with Robert Grant's Christian Cause in the mid-1970s and Jerry Falwell's Moral Majority in the 1980s. Fundamentalism now has been used to describe both Islamic fundamentalism and Jewish fundamentalism (Shahak & Mezvinsky, 1999; Ruthven, 2004; Sim, 2004). In each case, these fundamentalisms are a reaction to an atheistic modernism and advocate a return to Christian, Islamic, and Judaic values, law, and belief. In each case, this also implies a set of literalist convictions in relation to scripture or to sacred texts and a philosophical belief in the unmediated truth of the word. Literalism has a privileged place in these belief systems: language is always taken in a nonfigurative sense. In its strictest sense, scriptural literalism is a denial of allegory, parable, or metaphor. On this basis, fundamentalism often implies a set of beliefs in the onto-theological story of creation, man's nature and place, and the biological and social roles of men, women, and children. Scholars have applied the notion also to non-secular groups such as the militant animal rights activists, fundamentalist nationalisms or ethnicities such as Le Pen's National Front in France, and even neoliberals as "market fundamentalists" (Sim, 2004; Thompson, 2006).

This is a book written with the conviction that an appreciation of Derrida's work can shed some light on the growth of these fundamentalisms and on the new moralizers who based their authority on an unforgiving literalism and humanism. Derrida's work also reflects and engages with the tradition of Western metaphysics going back to Plato, promoting an understanding of the critique of *phallogocentrism* as a response to the Western philosophical tradition. Derrida systematically engages with the Western tradition with humanity, passion, and generosity and with patient and stunning scholarship. Phallogocentrism (along with logocentrism and Eurocentrism) refers to the privileging not just of European culture over all others but more deeply to the Western metaphysical tradition that holds to a hierarchy of values sustained by a binary logic that cannot do otherwise than privilege one term over another (reality/appearance, speech/writing, presence/absence, identity/difference, life/death). It is the general economy of an inherited humanism propping up all the ideological remnants of Man in his essence and all of the substitutions played out since Nietzsche that deconstruction seeks to destabilize, unmask, and undermine. Deconstruction, going beyond *Abbau* and *Destruktion*, works to undo "the metaphysics of presence" that holds that thought and speech (the *logos*) constitute the privileged center through which all discourse and meaning are derived. *Gott ist tot* (God is dead) is the shorthand that Nietzsche uses to proclaim this deepening of humanism. The "madman" in *The Gay Science* (Nietzsche, 1974) pronounces:

> God is dead. God remains dead. And we have killed him. How shall we comfort ourselves, the murderers of all murderers? What was holiest and mightiest of all that the world has yet owned has bled to death under our knives: who will wipe this blood off us? What water is there for us to clean ourselves? What festivals of atonement, what sacred games shall we have to invent? Is not the greatness of this deed too great for us? Must we ourselves not become gods simply to appear worthy of it? (Section 125)

God can no longer act as a source or foundation for moral authority, so what now can conceivably anchor the system of values? Nietzsche's observation heralds a new secularism in Europe and the end of the effective history of the church. At least, this is how Heidegger interprets it. The proposition "God is dead," as he says, has nothing to do with the assertion of an ordinary atheism. It means: "The supersensible world is without is effective power. It bestows no life. Metaphysics, i.e., for Nietzsche Western philosophy understood as Paltonism, is at an end" (Heidegger, 1977: 61). What would it mean to talk of Europe without God, or that the Christian God had become unbelievable, especially after the experiences of World Wars I and II? On what could a replacement code be based? Moral law derivable from our own rationality? (The beginning of liberal humanism with Kant). A kind of naturalism advocated by Hume, that is, a natural sympathy for others? Or should one give up on the search for foundations altogether and deny that moral codes and beliefs have any objective foundation. Perhaps they can be explained only psychologically? Nietzsche's works—especially his later writings: *Beyond Good and Evil* (1967a; orig. 1886), *On the Genealogy of Morals* (1967b; orig. 1887), *Twilight of the Idols* (1968; orig. 1888), *The Anti-Christ* (1968a; orig. 1888), *Ecce Homo* (1967c; orig. 1888)—initiate a radical strain of thought based on the observation that "God is dead" that informs the European avant garde (artists, writers, musicians) at the turn of the century and, thereafter, intellectuals in Germany and France in the postwar period: not only Freud, Heidegger, Adler, Jung, Mann, Scheler, Simmel, and Spengler but also Bataille, Camus, Sartre, Foucault, Deleuze, and Derrida.

Nietzsche's legacy is still very much a part of the contemporary intellectual landscape and he generates oppositions that define the context for the present debate about the role and status of the humanities. All the works of major philosophers have their "right" and "left" interpreters and defenders—this is true of Kant, Hegel, Nietzsche, and Wittgenstein (indeed, of Plato himself). The modern quarrel in the humanities has been read as a struggle over Nietzsche by a "right" Leo Strauss and a "left" Jacques Derrida. Peter Levine (1995: xviii–xix) argues that "Strauss and his followers are essentially duplicitous writers, holding an exoteric, conservative doctrine for the herd, and a esoteric, postmodern position for their *übermenschlich* readers." He argues that Alan Bloom and the Straussians are not genuine conservatives for they do not hold that the Western canon contains the accumulated wisdom of the Western tradition. By contrast, Levine argues that Derrida occupies the opposite end of the spectrum, a thinker who "saves" Nietzsche from Heidegger's reading of him as the "last metaphysician" only to herald Nietzsche as the first non-metaphysical thinker who helps to fashion Derrida's deconstructive practice recognizing that logocentrism or "the metaphysics of phonetic writing" is "a contingent but inescapable value" (p. 169).

Nietzsche is certainly central to the "quarrel" in the humanities today, and in a real sense we can take Strauss and Derrida as representing opposite ends of the spectrum. Bloom, sometimes classified with Yale deconstructionists in the 1970s (Paul de Man, Geoffrey Hartman, and J. Hillis Miller), was increasingly drawn to criticize deconstruction not merely on the basis of its interpretation of Nietzsche and to develop a conception of literature that differed from Derrida's.

> Deconstructionists emphasized the instability of linguistic meaning and the contradictions of conceptual thought, Bloom continued to champion the imagination's autonomy from

language, both literary and philosophic. To Bloom's thinking, literature is not the mind's play among unstable signs but the spirit's struggle for originality. (McPheron, 1998)

Bloom (1987: 379) described deconstruction as a "predictable...fad" based on a "cheapened interpretation of Nietzsche" and as "a dogmatic, academic nihilism of the Left" (Bloom, 1990: 28). In this connection, we should not forget that Nietzsche, Derrida and deconstruction, Foucault, and "postmodernism" were at the very heart of American debate surrounding the humanities during the chairmanship of the National Endowment for the Humanities by Lynne Cheney (wife of the vice president) from 1986 to 1993. *American Memory: A Report on the Humanities in the Nation's Public Schools* (Cheney, 1987) warned about the failure of schools to transmit knowledge of the past to future generations, and *Telling the Truth* (Cheney, 1996) examined the alleged effects of postmodernism and relativism in academia and politics.

Nietzsche's critique of morality—in particular his attack on prevailing conceptions of moral agency based on notions of free will, self-transparency, and moral sameness (one code applying universally to all)—begins to work historically to erode the moral certainty that invests Christian humanism and acts as a source of critique for those theorists who wish to expose the illusion of bourgeois morality or the thin veil of ignorance that cloaks religious teachings. It also informs an existentialist movement that flourishes in the 1940s and 1950s among Sartre, Beauvoir, Merleau-Monty, and Camus in France and Heidegger, Jaspers, and Buber in Germany, a broad cultural movement that attempts to rethink the problem of existence as a philosophical problem. Existentialism, in Sartre's famous phrase, is a humanism, and many who followed Nietzsche and/or Kierkegaard tended to give up on an objective or universal account of moral law or behavior to embrace a mode or way of being. Meaning is a product and outcome of existence, so no formal account can be given in advance and certainly not an account derived from the *nature* of human beings or indeed from any pre-given framework of ideas. Human existence cannot be approached in the same way as we approach things in terms of concepts or categories that we apply to understanding the external world. The question of self-description or self-examination or self-interpretation is crucial such that I cannot be dissociated from the account of what I am.

We have chosen to present Derrida as a *profound* humanist who committed to the value of truth and the promise of humanity endeavors to steer us away from its easy ideological fabrications that ultimately supports only a very tawdry and temporary cultural image of ourselves in one particular historical period. We present him so because he stands in a tradition not only within both contemporary modern traditions influenced by Nietzsche-Heidegger nexus and the immediate French tradition dating from Kojève's lectures on Hegel, but also in terms of the immediate inheritance from Sartre and his associates as well as Levinas, Blanchot, Althusser, and his many contemporaries including Deleuze, Lyotard, Kofmann, and Foucault. Clearly, one has to say the same of the modern tradition from Descartes and Kant, and, indeed, the tradition all the way back to Plato. We do not want to suggest a unity or origin of tradition but perhaps sustaining threads of a complex skein, and we must then also embrace the Hebraic tradition and various modern literary movements as well as those in the European avant garde. This chapter is entitled "Derrida as Profound Humanist," by which I mean that Derrida engages directly and systematically with the question of humanism—what it is to be human and what are its limits and boundaries in technology and animality—and with its continuance by some means: thus, a continuance through its encompassing of new extensions and mutations of rights in international law, in democracy to come, in the right to philosophize, in the author/writer/reader, in tasks for the new humanities, in an ethics of the Other—of hospitality—in the changed conditions for scholarship and media, in the promise of Europe in providing an alternative vision for world institutions and the governance of globalization. This is, in part, why we entertain the hypothesis "Deconstruction is a Humanism" with its ironical imitation of Sartre's authoritative dogmatic stance.

It is not entirely surprising that at the beginning of the twentieth first century two towering figures dedicate themselves to defining the meaning of humanism and attempt to renew humanistic scholarship: Jacques Derrida, an Algerian Jew, and Edward Said, a Palestinian Christian. Both immensely literate men are responsible, though in different ways, for altering the course of scholarship in the humanities and for introducing a new set of critical practices that mark out a philosophical extension and ethical revitalization of the meaning of literature, philosophy, and criticism. Through "orientalism," a concept that laid bare the ethnocentrism of Western assumption about the East, Said at once extended the work of Foucault and Derrida into the arena of postcolonial theory, demonstrating how exoticized and romantic images disguised the imperial basis of colonial rule. He argued how orientalism functions to harbor a persistent Western bias and prejudice against Arab Islamic peoples and their cultures. In essence, his work exposed the systematic alliance between the Enlightenment and colonialism while embracing a secular humanism himself that denied comfort to fundamentalists of all persuasions.

In 2001, when asked "What humanism is possible?" Said (2001) responded:

> the difficulty to begin with is that humanism in many ways is discredited. It has participated in, for example, systems like apartheid and colonialism that were exported to the non-European world by European thinkers and powers who thought they were doing humanism's work—civilizing the natives and brining the benefits of Western technology to the peripheries. And of course in this process they brought racial discrimination, racial hierarchies, and systems of exploitation, which were established in the interests of a humanism that said, "We are the bearers of an advanced culture and we should have the benefits of that even if it means subjugating lesser people." The whole concept of "lesser" civilizations and so on is, unfortunately, one of the burdens that humanism has to bear (n.d.).

In his posthumous work, *Humanism and Democratic Criticism*, Said (2005) defines humanism in a deconstructive way as "the practice of participatory citizenship" whose "purpose is to make more things available to critical scrutiny" and thus disclose its "human misreading and misinterpretations of a collective past and present" (p. 22). Said confirms that a form of humanism is still possible and his radical humanism draws on a form of democratic criticism based on self-knowledge, self-criticism, and the attempt to emancipate, enlighten, and educate.

Derrida, by comparison, also took on political work even although his detractors painted him as someone removed from the world of political action. Said himself dismissed Derrida's playfulness and insisted on the historical embeddedness of the text. Perhaps, Said was more committed to the rationalist tradition, to the individual, to philology, and to Vico's notion of self-knowledge and rhetoric. Yet both were displaced and both experienced the colonial condition early on. Both agree that humanism is not only still possible but also imperative, that we must search for viable forms that revitalize the humanities and reclaim for it a more active role in the public sphere.

There is no doubt that the humanities needs new tasks and Derrida has sought to provide a programmatic picture—that the humanities must also contextualize itself, escaping its local origins and trajectories, and broaden its account to take in the radical pluralism that exists as part of a new globalism that also recognizes the claims of local autonomy made by first peoples, indigenous peoples, sub-state cultural minorities, international religious movements, youth cultures, gender groups, and all sorts of political associations. Here the question of self and other looms large, as do questions revolving centrally around notion of ethics and politics. Derrida provides us with the rejuvenation of ancient concepts of friendship, the ethics of hospitality, forgiveness, the gift, and the invitation that outline his account of responsibility to the other.

We might say that the question emerging from the philosophy of the subject fundamentally concerns the question of agency. In Chapter 3, I assess the claims of the French anti-Nietzscheans who accuse Derrida of liquidating the subject. Derrida's establishment of deconstruction as an anti-Platonist machine for undoing metaphysics famously undermines a set of oppositional tendencies characteristic of the Western tradition. Deconstruction works best and is most easily exemplified in relation to specific texts. Here he demonstrates how the structure of writing is more significant than the priority accorded to speech by thinkers as diverse as Plato, Rousseau, Saussure, and Lévi-Strauss. Throughout his career, Derrida developed a series of related concepts and strategies— arche-writing, difference, trace, supplement—that enabled him to do the work of deconstruction, provided a new understanding of literature, and exerted a huge influence over the field of literary studies. His recent works such as *Archive Fever* (Derrida, 1995a) and *Paper Machine* (Derrida, 2005) examine the relationship between truth and authority, the question of memory, the architecture of the archive, machines for writing and the mechanization of writing, and the media in general in a world that is becoming increasingly digital and virtualized (see also Derrida 2002a, 2006).

Derrida has written extensively on the question of self and other, the author, the question of human and animal, and the question of technology in ways that lead some to criticize his alleged "anti-humanism," but Derrida attempts to deepen humanism by going beyond anthropological versions of humanism that do not question logocentrism or, indeed, the Eurocentrism that proceeds from it. Clearly, Derrida, as he himself puts it, is seeking the inspiration for a "new humanism." In his last interview, he maintains:

> What's more, since the beginning of my work, and this would be deconstruction itself, I have remained very critical with regard to Eurocentrism, to its formulation in modernist form, in the work of Valery, Husserl, or Heidegger, for instance. Deconstruction in general is a project that many have taken, rightly so, as an act of defiance toward all Eurocentrism. (Derrida, 2004: n.p.)

And yet there is also the promise of Europe and the European tradition and the new responsibility it must undertake to "sow the seed of a new post-globalization" that will transform the concept and practices of sovereignty and international law and also provide a ground for reflecting on social justice and secularism.

> Notwithstanding everything about the European tradition that can be deconstructed, it nonetheless remains that, precisely because of everything that has happened in Europe—because of the Enlightenment, because of the retrenchment of this little

continent, and of the enormous legacy of culpability that it bears (totalitarianism, nazism, genocides, Shoah, colonization and decolonization, etc.), today in the current geopolitical conditions in which we find ourselves, Europe, an entirely other Europe but with the same set of memories, could—or so I would wish—unite against the politics of American global dominance (see Wolfowitz, Cheney, Rumsfeld, etc.) and at the same time also against Arab-Muslim theocratism, unenlightened, and without a political future (but let's also take note of the diversity even in these two blocs, and let us ally ourselves with the opposition within them.). (Derrida, 2004: n.p.)

It is clear that Derrida sees himself in the tradition of the criticism initiated by Kant and demonstrated in the three critiques. He also views himself as wedded to the evolution or development of the Idea of Europe that, based on its permanent state of self-critique, offers the possibility of a humanism that is inclusive and free from racisms, from sexism, and from Eurocentrism:

"Deconstruction," even when it is directed against something European, is European, is a product of Europe, a reflection of Europe on itself as experience of a radical otherness. Since the days of the Enlightenment, Europe has been in a permanent state of self-critique, and in this tradition of perfectibility there is a hope for the future. At least I hope so, and this is what fuels my indignation before utterances that condemn Europe utterly, as if it were defined only by its crimes. (Derrida, 2004: n.p.)

This is a commitment to a promise, to a classically modern idea of freedom, and to a form of sovereignty that transcends the modern nation-state and the confines of national identity. It is a commitment also to broader political notions that define the new humanisms and the new humanities.

Note

1. Regarding the question of materialism, see the fragment of the letter from Houdebine, who provides Derrida with Lenin's formulation as the *taking of a position* in philosophy. See also Derrida's letter fragment where he maintains "Deconstruction...is not *neutral*. It *intervenes*" (p. 91 and p. 93, respectively).

References

Bloom, A. (1987) *The Closing of the American Mind*. New York: Simon and Schuster.
Bloom, A. (1990) "Western Civ," *Giants and Dwarfs: Essays 1960–1990*. New York: Simon and Schuster, Inc.
Cheney, L.V. (1987) *American Memory: A Report on the Humanities in the Nation's Public Schools*. Washington: National Endowment for the Humanities.

Cheney, L.V. (1996) *Telling the Truth: Why our Culture and Our Country Have Stopped Making Sense—and What We Can Do about It*. New York: Simon & Schuster.
Christian Delacampagne (2006) "The Politics of Derrida: Revisiting the Past," *MLN*, 121.4 862–871, at http://muse.jhu.edu/journals/mln/v121/121.4delacampagne01.html.
Derrida J. (1981) *Positions*. Alan Bass (trans.). Chicago: University of Chicago Press.
Derrida, J. (1982) "The Ends of Man," in *Margins of Philosophy*. Alan Bass (trans.). Chicago & London: Chicago University Press.
Derrida, J. (1983) "Punctuations: The Time of a Thesis," in *Philosophy in France Today*, Alan Montefiorie (ed.). Cambridge: Cambridge University Press.
Derrida, J. (1994) *Specters of Marx: The State of the Debt, the Work of Mourning, and the New International*, Peggy Kamuf (trans.). London: Routledge.
Derrida, J. (1995a) *Archive Fever: A Freudian Impression*, Eric Prenowitz (trans.). Chicago & London: University of Chicago Press.
Derrida, J. (1995b) *Points...Interviews, 1974–1994*. Stanford : Stanford University Press.
Derrida, J. (2001) "To Forgive: The Unforgivable and the Imprescriptible," in John D. Caputo, Mark Dooley & Michael J. Scanlon (eds.), Mark Dooley (trans.), *Questioning God*. Bloomington: Indiana University Press. pp. 21–51.
Derrida, J. (2002a) *Echographies of Television: Filmed Interviews*, with Bernard Stiegler, Jennifer Bajorek (trans.). Cambridge: Polity.
Derrida, J. (2002b) *On Cosmopolitanism and Forgiveness*, Mark Dooley & Michael Hughes (trans.). New York: Routledge.
Derrida, J. (2004) Jacques Derrida, The Last Interview. SV, at http://www.studiovisit.net/SV.Derrida.pdf. English translation of an interview given to *Le Monde* (August 19, 2004).
Derrida, J. (2005) *Paper Machine*, Rachel Bowlby (trans.). Stanford: Stanford University Press.
Derrida, J. (2006) *Geneses, Genealogies, Genres, and Genius: The Secrets of the Archive*, New York: Columbia University Press.
Heidegger, M. (1977) "The Word of Nietzsche; 'God is Dead'," in: *The Question Concerning Technology and Other Essays*. William Lovitt (trans.). Hew York: Harper & Row. pp. 53–112.
Levine, P. (1995) *Nietzsche and the Modern Crisis of the Humanities*. Albany: SUNY Press.
McPheron, W. (1998) Harold Bloom, Stanford's Presidential Lectures in the Humanities and Arts, at http://prelectur.stanford.edu/lecturers/bloom/.
Nietzsche, F. (1967a) *Beyond Good and Evil*, Walter Kaufmann (trans.). New York: Vintage Books.
Nietzsche, F. (1967b) *On the Genealogy of Morals*, Walter Kaufmann (trans.). NY: Vintage Books.
Nietzsche, F. (1967c) *Ecce Homo*, Walter Kaufmann (trans.). New York: Vintage Books.
Nietzsche, F. (1968) *Twilight of the Idols and The Antichrist*, R.J. Hollingdale (trans.). London: Penguin.
Nietzsche, F. (1974) *The Gay Science*, Walter Kaufmann (trans.). New York: Vintage Books.
Peters, M.A. (2001) "Politics and Deconstruction: Derrida, Neo-Liberalism and Democracy to Come," in Lawrence Simons & Heather Worth (eds.), *Derrida Downunder*. Palmerston North: Dunmore Press.
Ruthven, M. (2004) *Fundamentalism: The Search for Meaning*. Oxford: Oxford University Press.
Said, E. (2001) Interview: Edward Said on Humanism. Columbia Scholar to Receive Award and Give Lecture in Annandale by Kerry Chance, www.bard.edu/hrp/resource_pdfs/chance.said.pdf.
Said, E. (2005) *Humanism and Democratic Criticism*. New York: Columbia University Press.
Shahak, I. & Mezvinsky, N. (1999) *Jewish Fundamentalism in Israel*. London: Pluto Press.

Sim, S. (2004) *Fundamentalist World: The New Dark Age of Dogma*. Cambridge: Icon Books.
Simons, L. & Worht, H. (2001) (eds.), *Derrida Downunder*. Palmerston North: Dunmore Press.
Super, D.A. (2004) "The New Moralizers: Transforming the Conservative Legal Agenda," *Columbia Law Review*, 104.7: 2032–2096, http://www.columbialawreview.org/articles/index.cfm?article_id=736.
Thompson, G.F. (2006) Exploring Sameness and Difference: Fundamentalisms and the Future of Globalization, www.open.ac.uk/socialsciences/staff/gthompson/sameness_and_difference.pdf.
Trifonas, P. & Peters, M.A. (2004) *Deconstructing Derrida: Tasks for the New Humanities*. New York: Palgrave Macmillan.

· 3 ·

DERRIDA, NIETZSCHE, AND THE RETURN TO THE SUBJECT

MICHAEL A. PETERS

The assumption of one single subject is perhaps unnecessary; perhaps it is just as permissible to assume a multiplicity of subject, whose interaction and struggle is the basis of our thought and our consciousness in general? A kind of aristocracy of "cells" in which domination resides? To be sure, an aristocracy of equals, used to ruling jointly and understanding how to command? *My hypothesis*: The subject as multiplicity.
Friedrich Nietzsche, # 490, Book Three, "Principles of a New Evaluation," *The Will To Power*, W. Kaufmann & R.J. Hollingdale (trans.), W. Kaufmann (ed.), New York, Vintage Books, 1968, p. 270.

I believe that at a certain level both of experience and of philosophical and scientific discourse, one cannot get along without the notion of the subject. It is a question of knowing where it comes from and how it functions.
Jacques Derrida, from the discussion following "Structure, Sign and Play in the Discourses of the Human Sciences," in *The Structuralist Controversy*, Richard Macksey & Eugenio Donato (eds.), Richard Macksey (trans.), Baltimore, Johns Hopkins University Press, 1970, p. 271.

Introduction

Luc Ferry and Alain Renaut argue that "the philosophy of 68" eliminates and leaves no room for a positive rehabilitation of human agency necessary for a workable notion of democracy. In their Preface to the English Translation of *La pensée 68*, Ferry and Renaut (1990a: xvi) refer to the philosophy of the 1960s as a "Nietzschean-Heideggerian" antihumanism that is structurally incapable of taking up the promises of the democratic project inherent in modernity. Their criticisms are specifically aimed at Derrida and are intended as a path back to a form of humanism, liberalism, and individualism (the doctrine of human rights), which they think, can sustain a notion of political agency required for democracy.

Derrida provides us with resources for understanding and responding to these criticisms. He denies a simple-minded nihilism as it applies to the subject, to notions of political agency, and to the Idea of democracy and he argues that the anti-Nietzschean polemical attack on the critique of the subject is misplaced; that poststructuralism never "liquidated" the subject but rather rehabilitated it, decentered it, and repositioned it, in all its historical and cultural complexity. As he argues: "There has never been The Subject for anyone... The subject is a fable... but to concentrate on the elements of speech and *conventional* fiction that such a fable presupposes is not to stop taking it seriously (it is the serious itself)" (Derrida, 1995b: 264).

Derrida, Humanism, and Deconstruction

The American reception of deconstruction[1] and the influential formulation of "poststructuralism" in the English-speaking world quickly became institutionalized from the point at which Derrida delivered his essay "Structure, Sign and Play in the Discourse of the Human Sciences" to the International Colloquium on Critical Languages and the Sciences of Man at Johns Hopkins University in October 1966. Richard Macksey and Eugenio Donato (1970: x) described the conference as "the first time in the United States that structuralist thought had been considered as a cross-disciplinary phenomenon." Even before the conclusion of the conference, there were clear signs that the ruling transdisciplinary paradigm of structuralism had been superseded, yet only a paragraph in Macksey's "Concluding Remarks" signaled the importance of Derrida's "radical reappraisals of our [structuralist] assumptions" (p. 320).

In the now classic essay "Structure, Sign and Play," Derrida (1978a: 279–280) questioned the "structurality of structure" or notion of "center" which, he argued, has served to limit the play of structure:

> the entire history of the concept of structure... must be thought of as a series of substitutions of center for center, as a linked chain of determinations of the center.

> Successively, and in a regulated fashion, the center receives different forms or names. The history of metaphysics, like the history of the West, is the history of these metaphors and metonymies. Its matrix... is the determination of being as *presence* in all senses of this word. It could be shown that all the names related to fundamentals, to principles, or to the center have always designated an invariable presence—*eidos, arche, telos, energeia, ousia* (essence, existence, substance, subject) *aletheia*, transcendentality, consciousness, God, man, and so forth.

In this one paragraph, Derrida both called into question the previous decade of French structuralism and intimated the directions of his own intellectual ambitions. The decade of French structuralism, beginning with Claude Lévi-Strauss's (1958) *Anthropologie Structurale*, had its complex cultural prehistory in Nietzsche's critique of modernity, in the development of European structural linguistics, and in early twentieth-century modernism, especially formalism and futurism as it took form in both prerevolutionary Russia and Italy.[2]

The "decentering" of structure, of the transcendental signified, and of the *sovereign* subject—Derrida suggests, naming his sources of inspiration—can be found in the Nietzschean critique of metaphysics (especially, of the concepts of Being and truth) and in the Freudian critique of self-presence (as he says, "the critique of consciousness, of the subject, of self-identity and of self-proximity or self-possession" (ibid. 280), and, more radically, in the Heideggerian destruction of metaphysics, "of the determination of Being as presence" [ibid.]). In the body of the essay, Derrida considers the theme of "decentering" in relation to Lévi-Strauss' ethnology and concludes by distinguishing two interpretations of structure. One, Hegelian in origin and exemplified in Lévi-Strauss's work, he argues, "dreams of deciphering a truth or an origin which escapes play and the order of the sign" and seeks the "inspiration of a new humanism." The other, "which is no longer turned toward the origin, affirms play and tries to pass beyond man and humanism ..." (Derrida, 1978a: 292).

In another well-known essay "The Ends of Man," given as a lecture at an international colloquium in New York two years later (i.e., 1968), Derrida (1982: 114) addresses himself to the question of "where is France, as concerns man?" and he provides an account that interprets the dominant motif of postwar French philosophy as a philosophical humanism authorized by anthropologistic readings of Hegel, Marx, and Heidegger. Sartre's "monstrous translation" (p. 115) of Heidegger's *Dasein* legitimated an existentialist humanism, and even the critique of humanism, itself a major current of French thought in the postwar era, presented itself more as an amalgamation of Hegel, Husserl, and Heidegger with the old metaphysical humanism. Derrida argues: "the history of the concept man is never examined. Everything occurs as if the sign 'man' had no origin, no historical, cultural, or linguistic limit" (p. 116). This statement gives a strong indication as to Derrida's own motivations and directions: a movement towards an ever clearer specification of the subject in historical, cultural, and linguistic terms and an excavation of the history of the subject.[3]

Derrida reconsiders the *relève* of man in the thought of Hegel, Husserl, and Heidegger to demonstrate that in each case there is a clear critique of *anthropologism*. In particular, Heidegger's thought is guided by the double motif of being as presence and of the proximity of being to the essence of man (p. 128). He suggests that if we are not simply to restore the ordering of the system by taking recourse to humanist concepts or to destroy meaning, we face two strategic choices: either "to attempt an exit and a deconstruction without changing terrain, by repeating what is implicit in the founding concepts and the original problematic...," or "to decide to change terrain, in a discontinuous and irruptive fashion, brutally placing oneself outside, and by affirming an absolute break and difference" (p. 135). And he says, in an oft-quoted remark: "A new writing must weave and interlace these two motifs of deconstruction. Which amounts to saying that one must speak several languages and produce several texts at once" (ibid.). What we need to "change the terrain," he claims finally quoting Nietzsche, "is a change of 'style'; and if there is style, Nietzsche reminded us it must be *plural*" (ibid.).[4]

Derrida has never disowned the subject or its relevance either to philosophical or scientific discourse. He has, however, radically questioned the sovereign subject and the philosophical tradition of consciousness that left its indelible imprint on a variety of postwar humanisms. Inspired by Nietzsche and Heidegger, and befriended by Levinas, Derrida has interrogated the humanist construction of the sovereign subject—its genealogy and its authorial-functions—in his attempt to develop a science of writing that both deconstructs and moves beyond "man" as the full presence of consciousness in being. His work has been misinterpreted by those christening themselves anti-Nietzscheans who claim that Derrida (and post-structuralism in general) has "liquidated" or "eliminated" the subject and, therefore, endangered agency and posed a consequent threat to a workable notion of democracy. In this chapter, I briefly review the fierce attacks of the French "neoliberals" on Derrida and I elaborate the way Derrida provides us with resources for understanding and responding to these criticisms.

Antihumanism and the Metaphysics of the Subject

Luc Ferry and Alain Renaut published *La pensée 68* in 1985, poorly translated into English as *French Philosophy of the Sixties: An Essay on Antihumanism* (1990a). In the preface to the English translation, Ferry and Renaut maintain that French intellectual history since World War II has been dominated by "a critique of the modern world and the values of formal democracy" (p. xi) inspired by Marx and Heidegger that resulted in a common rejection of humanism. They claim that "Nietzschean-Heiggerianism" dates the advent of modern humanism from Descartes rather than from the rise of capitalism and works to "deconstruct" the subject defined as conscience and will, as "the author of his acts and ideas" (p. xii). In their description of the trajectory of French postwar thought, they assert that the critique of modern rationality was intimately bound up with the critique of the subject: Marxism had interrogated the universalism of the Enlightenment, based upon claims of the emancipation of man, in the light of Eurocentrism and European colonialism. When Marxism collapsed, the Heideggerian critique took over. They argue, "the retreat of Marxism has made the presence of Heideggerianism in France more and more visible" (p. xv) and that what happened to Marxism in the 1970s is happening to Heidegger today. In relation to both Marxism and Heideggerianism, they summarize their position thus:

> *Whether conducted in the name of a radiant future or a traditionalist reaction, the total critique of the modern world, because it is necessarily an antihumanism that leads inevitably to seeing in the democratic project, for example, in human rights, the prototype of ideology or the metaphysically illusion, is structurally incapable of taking up, except insincerely and seemingly in spite of itself, the promises that are also those of modernity* (p. xvi, italics in the original).

They claim that in their philosophical paradigm—what we can describe as a "French neoliberalism" (for the term, see Lilla, 1994)—it is necessary "to grant a minimum of legitimacy to a reference to the subject which is inherent in democratic thought" (p. xvi) and to bypass the confusion between metaphysics and humanism. It is, they claim, after Marx, Nietzsche, Freud, and Heidegger, today more than anything "a question of rethinking...the question of the subject" (p. xvi).

The antihumanism of French philosophy of the 1968 period is tracked out by reference to Derrida's "The Ends of Man," Foucault's declaration in *The Order of Things* of "the death of man," and Lyotard's skepticism of anthropologism.

Antihumanism holds that "the autonomy of the subject is an illusion" (p. xxiii) and that the problem that now confronts us, Ferry and Renaut suggest, "consists of searching for conditions for what a *nonmetaphysical humanism* might be" that involves "conferring a coherent philosophical status on the promise of freedom contained in the requirements of humanism" (p. xxviii). Ferry and Renaut wish to invent a form of modern humanism that is not metaphysical and permits the ascription of universal moral and political judgments and rights without further appeals to essentialist notions of human nature.

In this first attempt, Ferry and Renaut dissipate much of their energies by criticizing the Nietzschean-Hedeggerianism. While they legitimately question the Heideggerian critique of subjectivity—the meaning of the "metaphysics of subjectivity"—and inquire as to what can replace the metaphysical subject after its deconstruction (see p. 212), there are more rhetorical (and less savory) elements in their attack, which seek to damn Derrida and deconstruction by association with Heidegger's Nazism or Nietzsche's "irrationalism" and "illiberalism."[5] These rhetorical moves aside, there is little sustained engagement with Derrida's texts and their work seems excessively negative or mired in critique, without positively identifying, beyond the most schematic form, in what "modern humanism" might consist. For instance, toward the end of their book, they argue that "It does not follow that, having established that man is not really...autonomous..., one has to go to the extreme of withdrawing all meaning and function...from the Ideal of autonomy" (p. 211). Or, again, in the conclusion, they indicate that the critique of humanism and of the subject has revealed a "surprising" simplicity, suggesting that a *history of the subject* is yet to be written.

As Mark Lilla (1994) comments in respect to Ferry and Renaut,

> what they mean by the "subject" is often obscured in their writings, which up to now have mainly been critical and directed against their adversaries. They have yet to develop their own theory of subjectivity or respond to the objections that all such theories inevitably confront. Still it is clear what they wish such a theory of subjectivity to undergrid: a new defense of universal, rational norms in morals and politics, and especially a defense of human rights. (pp. 19–20)

Lilla clarifies that "such a defense would not be based upon the notion of an isolated individual as possessor of rights and, therefore, would not be compatible with classical liberalism" (p. 20). Instead, they appeal to a French republicanism that is to be articulated through a new humanism. To date this project has remained entirely programmatic and schematic and its content has been unfulfilled.[6]

The sorts of criticisms articulated by Ferry and Renaut represent a wider set a criticisms against Derrida and, more broadly, post-structuralism for its theoretical antihumanism and its alleged lack of a subject that can provide either for a notion of political agency and resistance or for the ascription of human rights and the workability of democracy. Indeed, strangely it is on the basis of this generalized criticism that liberals of all persuasions (old-fashioned thinkers, feminists, social democrats, and neoliberals) and humanist or disaffected structuralist Marxists and communitarians join hands. This new alliance can be given the generic term "anti-Nietzscheans." It is, perhaps, most obvious in the work of Ferry and Renaut (1991; Eng. Trans. 1997b), who in the early 1990s published a collection of essays with the title *Pourquoi nous ne sommes pas nietzschéens*, including essays by Vincent Descombes, Alain Boyer, and Phillippe Raynaud, among others. Yet it is also clear in the more general attack mounted against Derrida by Barry Smith, the editor of *The Monist* and the inaugurator of the infamous letter that sparked what Derrida called "the Cambridge Affair."[7] In the *Foreword* to a selection of essays edited by Smith (1994), for instance, he claims that the present ills facing American academic life are due directly to Foucault, Derrida, Lyotard, and others:

> Many current developments in American academic life—multiculturalism, "political correctness," the growth of critical theory, rhetoric and hermeneutics, the crisis of scholarship in many humanities departments—have been closely associated with, and indeed, inspired by, the work of European philosophers such as Foucault, Derrida, Lyotard and others. In Europe itself, in contrast, the influence of these philosophers is restricted to a small coterie, and their ideas have certainly contributed to none of the wide-ranging social and institutional changes we are currently witnessing in some corner of American academia.

This set of extraordinary claims are advanced without evidence of any kind; they are, after all, empirical statements rather than analytic ones, and, therefore, in terms Smith would accept, the establishment of their "truth" would necessarily require some historical evidence and analysis.

In the Smith (1994) collection, Dallas Willard (1994: 15) attempting to address the question of causation implied in Smith's assertions, concludes that to suppose that deconstructionism is *the* cause of the university crisis is a misdiagnosis. Yet he reiterates the charge in Smith's letter that deconstruction is not a *method* of thought. These are general attacks that do not proceed from a direct criticism of the Nietzscheanism assumed, often unproblematically, to exist as a source and inspiration for Derrida and to account for an antiliberalism in Derrida's thought (and that of other post-structuralists). The essay "The Decline and Fall of French

Nietzscheo-Structuralism" by Pascal Engel (1994) is a clearer example that echoes many of the criticisms raised by Ferry and Renaut. Engel (1994; 36–37, fn 3) distinguishes between what he calls Heideggero-Nietzscheanism (Derrida) and Metaphysical-Nietzscheanism (Deleuze) and formulates his criticisms in terms of a series of theses said to be the basis of Nietzscheo-Structuralism: there is no such thing as meaning, truth, epistemology (theses 1, 3, 4); nothing exists but forces (thesis 2); consciousness and subjectivity are just effects (of affects) (thesis 5); philosophy creates concepts (thesis 6). Engel (1994: 34) comments upon the "catastrophic consequences in political philosophy" of entertaining these theses (as if Deleuze or Derrida actually holds such crudely stated theses).

The new liberal alliance is also strongly evidenced in an essay by Charles Taylor (1994) on multiculturalism contributed to a collection edited by Amy Gutmann (1994), including Jürgen Habermas, K. Anthony Appiah, Susan Wolf, Micheal Walzer, and others. Taylor, for instance, at one point makes casual and off-hand remarks concerning "neo-Nietzscheans," referring to "subjectivist, half-baked neo-Nietzschean theories" (1994: 70). He mentions Derrida and Foucault only once and then without reference to specific texts and in derogatory terms.[8] Taylor argues that citizenship cannot be regarded as a basis for universal identity as people are both unique, self-creating individuals as well as bearers of culture. Both qualifications could easily be given a Nietzschean perspective, and, indeed, the question of cultural difference has been most thoroughly theorized, one might argue, by Derrida and a host of other post-structuralists (e. g., Foucault on micropractices, Lyotard on the *differend*, Deleuze on repetition and difference).

Derrida, for instance, constitutes an important place in the history of the subject when he invents the concept of *différance* and plots the linguistic limit of the subject. *Différance*, as Derrida (1981: 8–9) remarks, as both the common root of all the positional concepts marking our language and the condition for all signification, refers not only to the "movement that consists in deferring by means of delay, delegation, reprive, referral, detour, postponement, reserving" but also and finally to "the unfolding of difference," of the ontico-ontological difference, which Heidegger named as the difference between Being and beings.

Amy Gutmann (1994: 13) characterizes the concern for *cultural* difference and for the public recognition of particular cultures within liberal democracies as one that is forever counterbalanced by the concern for the protection of universal rights, and she translates the issue into the educational sphere as a dispute over the core curriculum and the content of courses when she sets up the debate in terms of the "essentialists" and the "deconstructionists." Gutmann (1994: 13–14) suggests that the "deconstructionists" argue:

> That to preserve the core by excluding contributions by women, African-Americans, Hispanics, Asians, and Native Americans as if the classical canon were sacred, unchanging, and unchangeable would be to denigrate the identities of members of these previously excluded groups and to close off Western civilization from the influences of unorthodox and challenging ideas of the sake of perpetuating sexism, racism, Eurocentrism, close-mindedness, the tyranny of truth (with a capital "T"), and a host of related intellectual and political evils.

To construct the debate in this way, as one between the opposite poles of essentialism and deconstructionism, allows Gutmann to safely impugn both and to come out on the side of liberal democracy. The debate over the core or multicultural curriculum is largely a reflection on the philosophy of the subject: essentialist or deconstructionist? There are a number of buried premises in the argument concerning the liberal theory of education and schooling, the education of reason, the shaping of selves, and so on. Gutmann does not make these theoretical connections. Whether she is kind to essentialists I will leave for others to judge. Her take on deconstructionists follows an analogous approach to the problem of agency argument: "deconstructionists erect a different obstacle to liberal democracy when they deny the desirability of shared intellectual standards, which scholars and students might use to evaluate our common education"; "they [deconstructionists] view common standards as masks for the will to political power of dominant, hegemonic groups" (p. 18). Gutmann asserts that such an argument is self-undermining, both logically and practically, for deconstructionism itself reflects the will to power of deconstructionists. Her quarrel with deconstructionism is that, first, "it denies *a priori* any reasonable answers to fundamental questions," and, second, "it reduces everything to an exercise of political power" (p. 20).

The difficulty is that Gutmann's "deconstructionists" are faceless; she never mentions Derrida or any theorist in association with deconstructionism. In other words, she sets up a straw man deconstructionism, which alleviates her of the scholarly *responsibility* to read or refer to specific texts, only to fiercely knock it down in the name of liberal democracy. We are entitled, for instance, to ask Gutmann: can Foucault really be considered a "deconstructionist"? Is the "will to power" a motivating concept in Derridean deconstruction or Foucauldian genealogy? Where does Derrida explicitly address the theme of ethnocentrism and what does he say concerning it? Gutmann has homogenized the differences between those she calls "deconstructionists" and while appropriating the term deconstructionism she has made no reference at all to Derrida's work. If Gutmann had investigated Derrida's work, she may have discovered that ethnocentrism and phallocentrism are seen to accompany the logocentrism that defines historically the attempt in the West to determine being as presence and that Nietzsche's influence, in Derrida's eyes, has been to free the signifier from the logos.[9]

In the *Preface* to the 1992 French edition, Ferry and Renaut (1997b: vii–viii) suggest that an appropriate retitling of the collection of essays might be "To think Nietzsche against Nietzsche" for they identify Nietzsche as the "inventor of the 'genealogy,'" the thinker, above all, who inspired the so-called master thinkers of the 1960s, who standing in the shadows of Nietzsche believed that they too could philosophize with a hammer, smashing the last idols of metaphysics and thereby moving beyond humanism. Yet, while they assert that "today nobody believes in Absolute Knowledge, in the meaning of history, or in the transparency of the Subject" (presumably the *thinking* of Nietzsche), it is also the case that "philosophy is not condemned to infinite deconstruction" (the thinking of Nietzsche *against* Nietzsche). They continue: "philosophy renews the ancestral desire for rationality, which the relativism of the modes of thought of difference invited us, too facilely, to renounce" (p. viii).

Only Vincent Descombes' (1997) essay deals with "Nietzsche's French Moment" and Descombes' analysis focuses upon Foucault and Deleuze to the exclusion of Derrida. Descombes generalizing to post-structuralism—(an "unnatural alliance" of Nietzscheanism with orthodox structuralism)—suggests that Nietzscheanism introduces no new principles apart from those of the "modern project" and its "critique of consciousness doesn't go beyond Cartesian mind philosophy" (p. 90). As he says, "The superior individual is inconceivable outside the idealist philosophy of autonomy" (p. 90).

Ferry and Renaut (1997a) bypass the so-called master thinkers or any one of them to concentrate on Nietzsche in relation to the question of democracy. They distinguish two attitudes to democracy: (1) the development or enlargement of the model of argumentative deliberation in either its theoretical or practical dimensions (Habermas, Apel, Rawls) and (2) the investigation of the possibility of the emergence of a contemporary analogue to a traditional universe through the development of the critique of democratic modernity (Strauss, MacInyre, and the "communitarians"—Taylor, Sandel, etc.). Nietzsche's case is interesting, they argue, especially in terms of critically investigating the neotraditionalist path because he articulates the critique of democratic modernity (and the argumentative foundation of democratic norms) while rejecting the neotraditionalist possibility of a contemporary analogue of tradition, in an age characterized by the death of God. This is an interesting and productive essay but one that hardly touches Derrida or Derrida's Nietzsche.[10]

Derrida's Response: "The Calculation of the Subject"

I shall argue that the anti-Nietzschean polemical attack on the critique of the subject is misplaced, for deconstruction and poststructuralism never "liquidated" the subject Rather it reassembled and reconstituted it, *after* deconstruction. While Ferry and Renaut talk of returning to the question of the subject, their critique of poststructuralism and their "non-metaphysical humanism" singularly lacks any resources for doing so. There is in Ferry and Renaut's work nothing that might suggest a reworking of the question of the subject in any guise except an innocent, historically naïve, and unproblematic return to a (neoliberal) human agency that chimes with the revitalization of *homo economicus*.

Jean-Luc Nancy (1991) comments in his "Introduction" to *Who Comes After the Subject?*

> I did not send my question ("Who comes after the subject?") to those who would find no validity in it, to those for whom it is on the contrary more important to denounce its presuppositions and to return, as though nothing had happened, to a style of thinking that we might simply call humanist, even where it tries to complicate the traditional way of thinking about the human subject (p. 3).

For Nancy, the contributors (including, Deleuze, Derrida, Blanchot, Lyotard, Levinas, Irigaray, Descombes, and many others) do not stand in a "tradition" or belong to a school, but rather "each entertains a complex rapport" to "the Husserlian, the Marxian, the Heideggerian, and the Nietzschean traditions" (p. 3). When Nancy writes of "those who return, as though nothing had happened, to the humanist subject," he clearly has in mind Ferry and Renaut.

In an interview with Nancy, Derrida (1995b: 256) disputes Nancy's interpretation of the "liquidation of the subject," and, discussing the discourse concerning "the question of the subject" in France over the last twenty-five years, suggests instead the slogan "a return to the subject, the return of the subject."[11] He begins the interview by briefly tracing the place of the subject in Lacan (the decentering of the subject), in Althusser (its interpellation), and in Foucault ("a history of subjectivity" and "a return to a certain ethical subject").[12]

> For these three discourses (Lacan, Althusser, Foucault) and for some of the thinkers they privilege (Freud, Marx, Nietzsche), the subject can be reinterpreted, re-stored, re-inscribed, it certainly isn't "liquidated." The question "who," notably in Nietzsche, strongly reinforces this point. This is also true of Heidegger, the principle reference or target of the *doxa* we are talking about. The ontological questioning that deals with the *subjectum*, in its Cartesian and post-Cartesian forms, is anything but a liquidation. (Derrida, 1995b: 257)

The attribution of the "liquidation" of the subject to a Nietzschean post-structuralism—an attribution underlying the polemical attacks of Ferry and Renaut and also of a French kind of neoliberalism—operates polemically to identify its target only by ignoring the time, place, and logical space of the subject, its multiple genealogy within the history of modern philosophy and its active reinterpretation and reinscription. What this tells us is that the *problematique* of the subject, as it has developed in France over the last twenty-five years, cannot be reduced to homogeneity.

Derrida's response to Nancy in the interview is both complex and detailed, covering extensive territory and raising fresh sources for inquiry. While it may be true to say that Derrida's discussion focuses upon an explication of themes in Heidegger (and Levinas to a lesser degree) in relation to a certain *responsibility* and the question of the subject, he makes reference to the entire history of the metaphysics of subjectivity, mentioning along the way many of the most prominent thinkers in the last twenty-five years of French philosophy. It is useful to consider Derrida's (1995b) description of the way in which the central "hegemony" of the subject was put into question again in the 1960s at a point when the question of time and of the other became linked to the interest in Husserl's discourse:

> It was in the 1950s and 1960s, at the moment when an interest in these difficulties [i.e., the dislocation of the absolute subject from the other and from time] developed in a very different way (Levinas, Tran-Duc-Thao, myself) and following moreover other trajectories (Marx, Nietzsche, Freud, Heidegger), that the centrality of the subject began to be displaced... But if certain premises are found "in" Husserl, I'm sure that one could make a similar demonstration in Descartes, Kant, and Hegel... This would have at least the virtue of de-simplifying, of "de-homogenizing" the reference to something like The Subject. (p. 264)

Derrida is turned to Heidegger by Nancy, and he refers to the act by which Heidegger substitutes a concept of *Dasein* for a concept of the subject simultaneously recalling "the essential ontological fragility of the ethical, juridical, and political foundations of democracy" (p. 266) that "remain essentially sealed within a philosophy of the subject" (p. 266). The question and task, Derrida suggests, is to develop an ethics, a politics, and an "other" democracy—he refers elsewhere to a "democracy to come" based upon Nietzsche's understanding (see below)—that is, "another type of responsibility" that would safeguard us against the "worst" *antidemocratic* intrusions (i.e., meaning National Socialism in all its forms). As Derrida (1995b) puts it:

> In order to recast, if not rigorously re-found a discourse on the "subject," on that which will hold the place (or replace the place) of the subject (of law, of morality, of politics—so many categories caught up in the same turbulence), one has to go through the experience of deconstruction (p. 272).[13]

Significantly, Derrida suggests that *Dasein*, in *Being and Time*, in spite of the questions it has raised and the spaces it has opened up for thinking, still occupies a place similar or analogous to that of the transcendental subject because it has been determined on the basis of a series of oppositions not sufficiently scrutinized. These oppositions include all the essential predicates of which subjects are the subject and which are ordered around being-present [*étant-present*] such as "presence to self…; identity to self, positionality, property, personality, ego, consciousness, will intentionality, freedom, humanity, etc." (p. 274). Derrida locates this responsibility in "that to which one *cannot and should not* submit the other in general"; in the "who" of friendship that provokes "conscience" and, therefore, opens up responsibility (p. 275). This "who" of friendship, he claims, belongs to the existential structure of *Dasein* and "precedes every subjectal determination" (p. 275), referring to both Nancy's *Inoperative Community* and Blanchot's *The Unavowable Community*. He says clearly:

> The origin of the call that comes from nowhere, an origin in any case that is not yet a divine or human "subject," institutes a responsibility that is to be found at the root of all ulterior responsibilities (moral, juridical, political), and of every categorical imperative. (Derrida, 1995b: 276)

This figure of responsibility can be approached also through Levinas's understanding of subjectivity of the *hostage* where "the subject is responsible for the other before being responsible for himself as 'me'" (p. 279).

While the discourses of Heidegger and Levinas disrupt a certain traditional humanism, they remain "profound humanisms *to the extent that they do not sacrifice sacrifice*" (p. 279). In other words, both thinkers tend to be humanists to the extent that only sacrifice of human life is forbidden, not life in general. Let me quote Derrida (1995b: 281–282) yet again—a tortuous passage but one that rescues (finally) the significance of the title "Eating Well" and casts light upon the remarks above.

> If the limit between the living and the nonliving now seems to be as unsure...as that between "man" and "animal," and if...the ethical frontier no longer rigorously passes between the "Thou shalt not kill" (man, thy neighbour) and the "Thou shalt not put to death the living in general,"...then, as concerns the "Good" [*Bien*] of every morality, the question will come back to determining the best, most respectful, most graceful, and also the most giving way of relating to the other and of relating the other to the self. For everything that happens at the edge of the orifices (of orality, but also of the ear, the eye—and all the "senses" in general) the metonymy of "eating well" [*bien manger*] would always be the rule.[14]

The explication of "who" in relation to sacrifice at once allows Derrida to emphasize the originality of Heidegger's and Levinas's discourses while recognizing their humanisms and the way they break from traditional humanism. (He suggests that Heidegger was a Judeo-Christian thinker). At the same time it allows Derrida to foreshadow the notion of responsibility for an ethics and politics to come that springs from the relation to the other.[15] Certainly it is the case, against Ferry and Renaut and other anti-Nietzscheans, that Derrida does not do away with the subject. He does not "eliminate" or "liquidate" although he does deconstruct the sovereign subject and the history of the subject. For Derrida—as his comment almost thirty years ago should remind us, a comment I have used to open this chapter—the notion of the subject is something one cannot get along without. It is never a question of doing without it so much as "knowing where it comes from and how it functions."

In relation to the question of democracy, Derrida (1994a: 41–42) resists the temptation to conclude that Nietzsche is an enemy of democracy in general and has nothing to offer in the name of "a democracy to come." His argument denies a simple-minded nihilism as it applies to the subject, to notions of political agency, and to the Idea of democracy: "Since, in my eyes, Nietzsche criticises a particular form of democracy in the name of 'democracy to come', I don't consider Nietzsche to be an *enemy of democracy in general*." Derrida suggests that this move is to open up the difference between a notion of democracy, "which while having something in common with what we understand by democracy today ...is reducible neither to the contemporary reality of "democracy" nor to the ideal of democracy informing this reality or fact." It is this difference that Derrida indicates he has explored at length in *Specters of Marx* (1994).

Although, as Derrida maintains, one cannot subscribe to all of what Nietzsche has written concerning the democracy of his day, he identified "particular risks in what he foregrounded under the name of 'democracy'" and "There are at the same time critical and genealogical motifs in Nietzsche which *appeal to a democracy to come*" (Derrida, 1994a: 41–42).

Richard Beardsworth observes that Derrida's work as distinct from both Nietzsche's and Heidegger's affirms both technology and democracy and asks the following question:

> Although the promise of democracy is not the same as either the *fact* of democracy or the regulative *idea* (in the Kantian sense) of democracy, deconstruction does "hear" *différance* more in a democratic organisation of government than in any other political model; and there are no new models to be invented. If I understand you correctly, your affirmation of democracy is, in this respect, a demand for the sophistication of democracy, such a refinement taking advantage, in turn, of the increasingly sophisticated effects of technology. (Derrida, 1994a: 18)

Beardsworth poses the question in relation to a number of pertinent observations: first, that "democratic institutions are becoming more and more unrepresentative in our increasingly technicized world"; second, that "the media are swallowing up the constitutional machinery of democratic institutions, furthering thereby the de-politicization of society and the possibility of populist demagogy"; third, that "resistance to this process of technicization is at the same time leading to virulent forms of nationalism and demagogy in the former Soviet empire," and; finally that "the rights of man would seem an increasingly ineffective set of criteria to resist this process of technicization (together with its possible fascistic effects) given this process's gradual effacement of the normative and metaphysical limit between the human and the inorganic" (p. 18).

Derrida responds by contemplating the nature of contemporary acceleration of technicization and the relation between technical acceleration—a product of the so-called technosciences—and politico-economic processes, which relate rather to the structure of decision making. In relation to these two kinds of acceleration, Derrida asks, "what is the situation today of democracy?" His response is worthy of noting:

> "Progress" in arms-technologies and media-technologies is incontestably causing the disappearance of the site on which the democratic used to be situated. The site of representation and the stability of the location which make up parliament or assembly, the territorialisation of power, the rooting of power to a particular place, if not to the ground as such—all this is over. The notion of politics dependent on this relation

between power and space is over as well, although its end must be negotiated with. I am not just thinking here of the present forms of nationalism and fundamentalism. Technoscientific acceleration poses an absolute threat to Western-style democracy as well, following its radical undermining of locality. Since there can be no question of interrupting science of the technosciences, it's a matter of knowing how a democratic response can be made to what is happening. This response must not, for obvious reasons, try to maintain at all costs the life of a democratic model of government which is rapidly being made redundant. If technics now exceeds democratic forms of government, it's not only because assembly or parliament is being swallowed up by the media. This was already the case after the First World War. It was already being argued then that the media (then the radio) were forming public opinion so much that public deliberation and parliamentary discussion no longer determined the life of a democracy. And so, we need a historical perspective. What the acceleration of technicisation concerns today is the frontiers of the nation-state, the traffic of arms and drugs, everything that has to do with inter-nationality. It is these issues which need to be completely reconsidered, not in order to sound the death-knell of democracy, but in order to rethink democracy *from within these conditions*. (Derrida, 1994a: 57–58)

Derrida maintains that since technics have obliterated "locality," the future of democracy must be thought in global terms. It is no longer possible to be a democrat "at home" and wait to see what happens "abroad." In emphasizing the call to a world democracy, Derrida suggests that the stakes of a "democracy to come" can no longer be contained within frontiers or depend upon the decisions of a group of citizens or a nation, or group of nations. The call is for something new that is both more modest and yet also more ambitious than any overriding concept of the universal, the cosmopolitan, or the human. Derrida distinguishes between a rhetorical sense of democracy as politics that transcends borders (as one might speak of the United Nations) and what he calls a "democracy to come." The difference exhibits itself in decisions made in the name of the Rights of Man that, he suggests, "are at the same time alibis for the continued inequality between singularities." He indicates that we need to invent new concepts—concepts other than that of "state," "superstate," "citizen," and so forth—for what he has called the new International (Derrida, 1993). He says:

> The democracy to come obliges one to challenge instituted law in the name of an indefinitely unsatisfied justice, thereby revealing the injustice of calculating justice whether this be in the name of a particular form of democracy or of the concept of humanity. (Derrida, 1994a: 60–61)

Elsewhere Derrida (1994b) explains what he means by deconstructing the foundations of international law. While international law is a good thing, it is nevertheless rooted in the Western concept of philosophy—as he says, "in its mission, its axiom, in its languages"—and the Western concept of state and sovereignty, which acts as a limit. In order to rethink the international order and think of a "democracy to come," we must deconstruct the foundations of international law and the international organizations built upon it. The second limit is that the international organizations are governed by a number of powerful rich states, including the United States.

Derrida here is attempting "to deconstruct the political tradition not in order to depoliticize but in order to interpret differently the concept of the political."

> So justice and gift should go beyond calculation, which doesn't mean that we shouldn't calculate, we should calculate it as rigorously as possible but there is a point or a limit beyond which calculation must fail ... And so what I tried to think or to suggest is a concept of the political and of democracy which would be compatible, which could be articulated with these impossible notions of the gift and justice. (Derrida, 1994b)

It might be argued that the prospect of a critical pedagogy of difference, of a genuinely multicultural and internationalist pedagogy suitable for the future, is located at the interstices and in the interplay between a "democracy to come" and a "subject to come," a global subject whose critical function it is to both initiate and interrogate the new International.

Notes

1. For a clear account of deconstruction and its American reception and mediation (especially at the hands of Paul de Man) as a school of literary criticism, see Rorty (1995). Rorty provides an exemplary account of both deconstructionist theory and the two main lines of (analytic) criticism against Derridean philosophy.
2. See my "Poststructuralism and the Philosophy of the Subject," Chapter 1, in Peters (1996).
3. Judith Butler's (1987: 175) comment is entirely apposite here: "The twentieth-century history of Hegelianism in France can be understood in terms of two constitutive moments: (1) the specification of the subject in terms of finitude, corporeal boundaries, and temporality and (2) the 'splitting' (Lacan), 'displacement' (Derrida), and eventual death (Foucault, Deleuze) of the Hegelian subject."
4. For an account on the importance of Nietzsche to Derrida see his *Spurs* (Derrida, 1978b), and of Nietzsche to poststructuralist thought see Behler (1991), Large (1993), and Schrift (1995; 1996).
5. See, for example, their reference in the preface to the English translation, to Victor Farias (p. xv). They also later became embroiled in the so-called Heidegger affair when Farias's book sparked a debate in the 1980s concerning alleged new revelations of Heidegger's Nazi involvement. See Ferry and Renaut's (1990b) *Heidegger and Modernity*.

6. Lilla (1994: 32, fn38) makes the following useful remark:

   Ferry and Renaut have made two, not always compatible appeals to previous philosophies of the subject. One is to Kant, and specifically to the *Critique of Judgment*, wishing to avoid the transcendental presuppositions of the First Critique and the rigors of the Second, they have followed the increasingly common strategy of seeking in the Third an "aesthetic" model for reflection on morals and politics... A second appeal is to Fichte, specifically to his earliest work: here they discover a "non-metaphysical" philosophy of the subject that makes room for intersubjective experience and permits a critical analysis of history.

   The first appeal might be considered curious in the light of the fact that Lyotard first moved in this direction in the early 1980s to sustain his notion of heterogenous language games. See his essay "Answering the Question; What is Postmodernism?" an appendix to *The Postmodern Condition* (1984).
7. For the full text of the letter and Derrida's response, originally published in the *Cambridge Review* in 1992, see Derrida's (1995a) "*Honoris Causa*: 'This is *also* extremely funny.'" For a recent and balanced account of the affair, see Joseph Margolis (1994).
8. For a full discussion of this matter see "Monoculturalism, Multiculturalism and Democracy: The Politics of Difference or Recognition?" Chapter 10 in Peters (1996).
9. See, for example, Derrida's (1976: 19) comment: "Radicalizing the concepts of *interpretation, perspective, evaluation, difference*, and all the 'empiricist' or nonphilosophical motifs that have constantly tormented philosophy throughout the history of the West, and besides, have had nothing but the inevitable weakness of being produced in the field of philosophy, Nietzsche, far from remaining simply (with Hegel and as Heidegger wished) within metaphysics, contributed a great deal to the liberation of the signifier from its dependence or derivation with respect to the logos and the related concept of truth or the primary signified, in whatever sense that is understood." Derrida begins the "Exergue" to his *Of Grammatology* by focusing our attention on the ethnocentrism that has controlled our notion of writing and addresses the notion further in *Part II Nature, Culture Writing*. This would be an appropriate starting point for Gutmann if she was interested in "deconstructionism" in relation to the question of ethnocentrism. Still the best short commentary, in my view, on Derrida in relation to Nietzsche, Heidegger, and Freud is Gayatri Chakravorty Spivak's (1976) "Translator's Preface" to *Of Grammatology*.
10. Of all the essays, perhaps, the most interesting and most relevant for my purposes here is Phillippe Raynaud's (1997) "Nietzsche as Educator." Raynaud wants to approach Nietzsche's oeuvre directly rather than through his "French admirers" to ask about the kind of philosophy possible today, Nietzsche's relation to the Enlightenment and his critique of modern ideals. His interpretation is, I think, insightful: "The task for democratic political thinking is analogous to that which I have tried to define for philosophy: as an antidote to the modern spirit, Nietzsche's thought should be taken by modernity as a privileged means for self-criticism. It is in that respect, more than as a master of truth, that Nietzsche is an *educator*."
11. The interview with Jean-Luc Nancy entitled "'Eating Well,' or The Calculation of the Subject" was originally published in *Cahiers Confrontation* 20 (Winter 1989), an issue called "Après le subjet qui vent" (After the subject who comes). All references in this chapter are to the full interview now published in *Points... Interviews, 1974–1994* (Derrida, 1995b).

12. Derrida (1995b: 256) notes, "As for Foucault's discourse, there would be different things to say according to the stages of its development." This remark is important for it reveals the complexity of the question of the subject in the thought of *one* thinker that demonstrates the inadequacy of the generalized description of the "liquidation" of the subject as it applies to the whole of postwar French philosophy.
13. Invoking a certain notion of *responsibility* that is excessive in that it "regulates itself neither on the principles of reason not on any sort of accountancy," Derrida (1995b: 272) suggests that the subject is also "a principle of calculability"—hence part of the title of the interview "The Calculation of the Subject." As he suggests "the subject is also a principle of calculability—for the political (and even, indeed, for the current concept of democracy, which is less clear, less homogenous, and less of a given than we believe or claim to believe, and which no doubt needs to be rethought, radicalized, and considered as a thing of the future), in the question of legal rights (including human rights, about which I would repeat what I have just said about democracy) and in morality" (Derrida, 1995b: 272). Yet, for us to arrive at a notion of responsibility that might carry with it the new possibilities and new meanings for the political and the moral, the calculation of the subject must pass through deconstruction.
14. The translators note (Note 15, p. 475) says: "The phrase in play here, 'Il faut bien manger' (which is also the original title of the interview), can be read in at least two ways: 'one must eat well' or 'everyone has to eat'. In addition, when the adverb 'bien' is nominialized as 'le Bien', there results the sense of 'eating the Good.' It is this multivalent sense that Derrida explores in the succeeding sentences." I shall not attempt to précis Derrida's stunning and surprising "turns" but will simply leave it as an enticement.
15. I think it is useful to refer to the way in which Derrida recognizes how the question of the subject and of the living "who," as he says, is at the heart of the most pressing concerns of modern societies. I shall summarize: decisions over birth and death involving the treatment of sperm or ovum, surrogacy, genetic engineering, bioethics, biopolitics, euthanasia, organ removal, and transplant.

References

Behler, E. (1991) *Confrontations: Derrida, Heidegger, Nietzsche*, S. Taubeneck (trans.). Stanford, CA: Stanford University Press.

Cadava, E., Connor, P. & Nancy, J.-L. (eds.) (1991) *Who Comes After the Subject?* New York: Routledge.

Derrida, J. (1976) *Of Gammatology*, G.C. Spivak (trans.). Baltimore and London: Johns Hopkins University Press.

Derrida, J. (1978a) "Structure, Sign and Play in the Discourses of the Human Sciences," in A. Bass (trans.), *Writing and Difference*. Chicago: University of Chicago Press. pp. 278–293.

Derrida, J. (1978b) *Spurs: Nietzsche's Styles*, B. Harlow (trans.). Chicago: Chicago University Press.

Derrida, J. (1981) *Positions*, A. Bass (trans.). Chicago: University of Chicago Press.

Derrida, J. (1982) "The Ends of Man," in A. Bass (trans.), *Margins of Philosophy*. Chicago: University of Chicago Press. pp. 109–136.

Derrida, J. (1983) "The Time of the Thesis: Punctuations," in Alan Montefiore (ed.), *Philosophy in France Today*. Cambridge: Cambridge University Press. pp. 34–50.

Derrida, J. (1985) "Octobiographies: The Teaching of Nietzsche and the Politics of the Proper Name," in Avital Ronell (trans.). *The Ear of the Other: Otobiography, Transference, Translation*, Christie V. McDonald, Peggy Kamuf (trans.). New York: Schocken Books. pp. 1–38.

Derrida, J. (1994a) "Nietzsche and the Machine: An Interview with Jacques Derrida by Richard Beardsworth," *Journal of Nietzsche Studies*, 7: 7–66.

Derrida, J. (1994b) "Roundtable Discussion with Jacques Derrida," J. Christian Guerrero (trans.), Villanova University, October 3. Located at: http://www.lake.de/home/lake/hydra/vill1.html.

Derrida, J. (1995a) "*Honoris Causa*: 'This is *also* extremely funny,'" in E. Weber (ed.), P. Kamuf & others (trans.), *Points...Interviews, 1974–1994*. Stanford, CA: Stanford University Press. pp. 399–421.

Derrida, J. (1995b) "'Eating Well', or the Calculation of the Subject," in E. Weber (ed.), P. Kamuf & others (trans.), *Points...Interviews, 1974–1994*. Stanford, CA: Stanford University Press. pp. 255–287.

Derrida, J. (1995c) "Is There a Philosophical Language?" in E. Weber (ed.), P. Kamuf & others (trans.), *Points...Interviews, 1974–1994*. Stanford, CA: Stanford University Press.

Descombes, V. (1997) "Nietzsche's French Moment," in Ferry, L. & Renaut, A. (eds.), R. de Loaiza (trans.), *Why We Are Not Nietzscheans*. Chicago & London: University of Chicago Press. pp. 70–91.

Descombes, V. (1980) *Modern French Philosophy*, L. Scott-Fox & J. Harding (trans.). New York: Cambridge University Press.

Dreyfus, H. (1998) "Heidegger and Foucault on the Subject, Agency and Practices," Unpublished paper.

Ferry, L., & Renaut, A. (1990a) *French Philosophy of the Sixties. An Essay on Antihumanism*, M. Cattani (trans.). Amherst: University of Massachusetts Press.

Ferry, L., & Renaut, A. (1990b) *Heidegger and Modernity*, Franklin Phillip (trans.). Chicago: Chicago University Press.

Ferry, L., & Renaut, A. (1991) *Pourquoi nous ne sommes pas nietzschéens*. Paris: Éditions Grasset & Fasquelle.

Ferry, L., & Renaut, A. (1997a) "What Must First Be Proved Is Worth Little," in Ferry, L. & Renaut, A. (eds.), *Why We Are Not Nietzscheans*, R. de Loaiza (trans.). Chicago & London: University of Chicago Press. pp. 92–109.

Ferry, L., & Renaut, A. (eds.) (1997b) *Why We Are Not Nietzscheans*, R. de Loaiza (trans.). Chicago and London: University of Chicago Press.

Large, D. (1993) "Translator's Introduction" to Sarah Kofman, *Nietzsche and Metaphor*. London: Athlone Press. pp. vii–xl.

Leitch, V. (1996) *Local Effects, Glocal Flows*. New York: State University of New York Press.

Levi-Strauss, C. (1958) *Anthropologie structurale*. Paris : Pocket.

Macksey, R. & Donato, E. (eds.) (1970) *The Structuralist Controversy: The Languages of Criticism and the Sciences of Man*. Baltimore & London: Johns Hopkins University Press.

Margolis, J. (1994) "Deferring to Derrida's Difference," in Barry Smith (ed.), *European Philosophy and the American Academy*. La Salle, IL: Hegeler Institute, Moinst Library of Philosophy. pp. 195–226.

Nancy, J.-L. (1991) "Introduction," in E. Cadava, P. O'Connor, & J.-L. Nancy (eds.), *Who Comes After the Subject?* London and New York: Routledge. pp. 1–8.

Peters, M. (1996) *Poststructuralism, Politics and Education*. Westport, CT and London: Bergin & Garvey.

Peters, M. (1998) "Introduction: Naming the Multiple," in M. Peters (ed.), *Naming the Multiple: Poststructralism and Education*. Westport, CT and London: Bergin & Garvey.

Peters, M. (2003) "Derrida, Pedagogy and the Calculation of the Subject," in P. Trifonas (ed.), *Pedagogies of Difference*. New York & London: RoutledgeFalmer.

Raynaud, P. (1997) "Nietzsche as Educator," in Ferry, L. & Renaut, A. (eds.), R. de Loaiza (trans.), *Why We Are Not Nietzscheans*. Chicago and London: University of Chicago Press. pp. 141–157.

Rorty, R. (2005) "Deconstruction," in Raman Selden (ed.), *The Cambridge History of Literary Criticism*, Vol. 8, *From Formalism to Poststructuralism*. Cambridge: Cambridge University Press.

Schrift, A. (1995) *Nietzsche's French Legacy: A Genealogy of Poststructuralism*. New York and London: Routledge.

Schrift, A. (1996) "Nietzsche's French Legacy," in B. Magnus & K. Higgins (eds.), *The Cambridge Companion to Nietzsche*. Cambridge: Cambridge University Press. pp. 323–355.

Spivak, G.C. (1976) "Translator's Preface," to J. Derrida, *Of Grammatology*. Baltimore and London: Johns Hopkins University Press.

Trifonas, P. (1998) "Jacques Derrida: The Ends of Pedagogy—from the Dialectic of Memory to the Deconstruction of the Institution," in Peters, M. (ed.), *Naming the Multiple: Poststructuralism and Education*. Westport, CT, and London: Bergin and Garvey.

Ulmer, G. (1985) *Applied Grammatology: Post(e)-Pedagogy from Jacques Derrida to Joseph Beuys*. Baltimore: Johns Hopkins University Press.

· 4 ·

FROM CRITIQUE TO DECONSTRUCTION:
DERRIDA AS A CRITICAL PHILOSOPHER

GERT BIESTA

> Deconstruction, if such a thing exists, should open up.
>
> *(Derrida, 1987: 261)*

In 1991, Emmanuel Levinas wrote the following about Derrida:

> May not Derrida's work cut into the development of Western thinking with a line of demarcation similar to that of Kantianism, which separated dogmatic philosophy from critical philosophy? Are we again at the end of a naïveté, of an unsuspected dogmatism which slumbered at the base of that which we took for critical spirit? (Levinas, 1991: 3)

Levinas's observations are a good place to begin this chapter for they suggest that "deconstruction"—the not-totally-correct-name under which Derrida's work has become known—occupies a special place in the tradition of critical philosophy. One could, of course, argue that *all* Western philosophy is critical philosophy. After all, ever since philosophy has lodged itself into Western thought, it has understood itself as a critical enterprise. Socrates is undoubtedly the main icon of the critical style of philosophy. Plato "translated" the Socratic approach into a distinction between knowledge (*episteme*) and belief (*doxa*). This not only served as a formalization of the Socratic style, it also entailed a division of tasks—and thereby a distinction—between the common man, who could achieve only *doxa*, and the philosopher, who could have *episteme*, who could have knowledge of an ultimate reality beyond mere convention and decision. Apart from a justification of the superior position of the philosopher in the *polis*, Plato's distinction also articulated a specific understanding of the *resources* for critique. For Plato it was knowledge of ultimate reality, that is, of the world of Ideas, that would provide the philosopher with a *criterion* so that *krinein*—distinction, separation, decision, disputation, judgment—would become possible. In a similar vein, Aristotle stressed the indispensability of a criterion. "There must be certain canons," he wrote, "by reference to which a hearer shall be able to criticize" (Aristotle, *De Partibus Animalium*, I.1, 639a: 12).

While Western philosophy has traveled many different routes since Socrates, Plato, and Aristotle, the critical impetus has not been lost. It seems more accurate to say that the critical motive has become *a*, if not *the*, central concern for modern philosophy, especially since it had to renounce its claim to a higher form of knowledge about the natural world as a result of the emergence of modern natural science (see Rorty, 1980). A crucial step in the development of the critical phase of modern philosophy was the *generalization* of the idea of critique. Pierre Bayle—the "other" philosopher from Rotterdam—was among the first modern scholars who went beyond the idea that only texts could be the object of critique (see his *Dictionaire Historique et Critique* from 1715). From then on institutions such as church and state, and society more generally, became possible targets for critical examination (see Röttgers, 1990). This culminated, a few decennia later, in Kant's bold claim that our age is "the true age of critique," a critique "to which everything must be subjected" (see Röttgers, 1990: 892).

Kant's three *Critiques* still stand out as a major attempt to articulate what it could mean for philosophy to be critical. But Kant has not said the last word. His idea of critique as a tribunal of reason was challenged by Hegel and Marx from a perspective in which a much more historical orientation came to the fore (see Röttgers, 1990). Both orientations—reason and history—have continued to play a central role in the two main critical traditions of twentieth-century philosophy: Popper's critical rationalism and the critical theory of the Frankfurt School.

Within education, one of the most explicit manifestations of the role of critique has been developed in the area of critical thinking. Robert Ennis's 1962-article "A Concept of Critical Thinking" (Ennis, 1962) is often credited as the starting point for the present interest in critical thinking in the English-speaking world (see, e.g., Siegel, 1988: 5; Thayer-Bacon, 1993: 236; Snik & Zevenbergen, 1995: 103). In his article, Ennis defined critical thinking as "the correct assessing of statements" (Ennis, 1962: 83) and identified several aspects and dimensions of critical thinking. In later publications, Ennis revised his definition to "reasonable reflective thinking that is focused on deciding what to believe or do" (Ennis, 1987: 10), arguing that one must have both the skills necessary to be a critical thinker and the inclination to use these skills.

Ennis's work has not only been an important factor in the resurgence of interest in critical thinking as an educational ideal. It has also provided an important point of reference for subsequent debates concerning critical thinking and education. Although more "traditional" questions about the nature and scope of critical thinking continue to surface, one issue that has become increasingly central in recent years is the question as to whether the idea(l) of critical thinking is a neutral, objective, universal, and self-evident idea(l), or whether it is in some way biased (e.g., by culture, class, or gender). Although the bias-question is part of the more general question concerning the justification and justifiability of the idea(l) of critical thinking,[1] it is special in that it has not so much emerged from the internal development of the debate about critical thinking but mainly from the ways in which the idea(l) of critical thinking has been challenged from the "outside." Postmodernist, feminists, and (neo-)pragmatists are among those who have questioned the neutral, self-evident character of the idea(l) of critical thinking.[2] They have not done this, so it must be stressed, in order to reject the idea(l), but rather to come to a more encompassing articulation—a "redescription" (Thayer-Bacon, 1998)—of it.

Any answer to the question whether or not the idea(l) of critical thinking is biased is intimately connected with the way in which we conceive of the idea of critique itself. It is intimately connected, in other words, with our conception of "criticality." The purpose of this chapter is not only to show that the question as to what it means to be critical can be answered in different and clearly distinguishable ways. I also wish to make clear how and in what way deconstruction can be understood as a form of critical philosophy and how Derrida's "quasi transcendentalism" compares to other traditions of critique and notions of criticality. To do so, I will compare deconstruction with two conceptions of criticality to which I will refer as "critical dogmatism" and "transcendental critique" respectively. These conceptions, which represent major positions in contemporary philosophy, differ not only in their understanding of what it means to be critical—which means that they entail different definitions of the critical "operation." They also rest upon different *justifications* for being critical. They provide, in other words, different answers to the question as to what gives each of them the "right" to be critical.

Critical Dogmatism

The first way to understand what it means to be critical is to think of critique as the application of a criterion in order to evaluate a specific state of affairs. I propose to refer to this "style" of critique as critical dogmatism (see below). The "operation" can be called critical in that it gives an evaluation of a specific state of affairs. Yet the operation is dogmatic in that the criterion itself is kept out of reach of the critical operation. Critical dogmatism, so we could say, derives its right to be critical from the truth of the criterion. In education, we can find many examples of this style of critique. Critical work is, for example, carried out by means of a definition of what counts as education (see, e.g., Peters, 1966). Such a definition can then be used to evaluate educative practices and theories that can then turn out be, for example, non-educative or indoctrinary. A further example can be found in the work of those educators who take "emancipation" as the general criterion for the evaluation of educational theory and practice, as is the case in critical pedagogy.

Although I refer to this style of critique as a dogmatic approach, there is, as such, nothing objectionable to it. That is to say, there is nothing objectionable as long as one recognizes and accepts its dogmatic character. In his *Treatise on Critical Reason* (Albert, 1985), Hans Albert has even suggested that critical dogmatism is inevitable. He argues, in what has become known as the *Münchhausen trilemma*, that any attempt to articulate foundations—and in critical dogmatism, the criterion is the foundation of the critical operation—inevitably leads to a trilemma, that is, "a situation with three alternatives, all of which appear unacceptable" (Albert, 1985: 18). According to Albert, we are forced to choose (1) an infinite regress, because the propositions that serve as a fundament need to be founded themselves; (2) a logical circle that results from the fact that in the process of giving reasons one has to resort to statements that have already shown themselves to be in need of justification; or (3) breaking off the attempt at a particular point by dogmatically installing a foundation. Since neither the first nor the second option appears to lead to any satisfactory results in finding and founding a criterion, the conclusion can only be, so Albert argues, that the only possible foundation for critique is a dogmatic foundation, so that the only possible form of critique is critical dogmatism.

While there may be good reasons for conceiving of critique as criterion-based evaluation, it is not difficult to see that there is at least a tension and possibly even a contradiction at stake in this conception of criticality. All depends, of course, on whether one accepts Albert's conclusion that the basis for critique can be only conventional. Although I do not wish to suggest that the application of certain criteria has never had any positive effects or that any critical work along these lines has been in vain, the contradiction entailed in critical dogmatism is, of course, problematic—not in the least for a philosophy that aims to be critical. The question of whether it is possible to overcome the dogmatic foundation of critical philosophy has been answered in the affirmative by a position to which I will refer as "transcendental critique."

Transcendental Critique

Like critical dogmatism transcendental, critique conceives of the critical operation as the application of a criterion. The main difference between the two critical approaches, however, lies in the way in which this criterion is justified. The transcendental style of critique must be understood against the background of the way in which philosophy had to reconsider its position as a result of the emergence of the scientific worldview. From then onwards, philosophy could no longer claim to provide knowledge of the natural world, nor could it claim to provide knowledge of a more fundamental reality (metaphysics). As a result, it lost its role as a foundational discipline. It was Kant who put philosophy on a new track—transcendental philosophy—in which it became the proper task of philosophy to articulate the conditions of possibility of true (scientific) knowledge (and, within the Kantian project, also of true metaphysical knowledge, that is, knowledge of the synthetic judgments a priori; see Kant, 1956).

Although transcendental philosophy opened up a whole new field for modern philosophy, Kant's program was almost immediately criticized for the reflexive paradox it contained. It was Hegel who exposed the problematic character of the attempt to acquire knowledge of something of which the existence had already to be presupposed (the capacity to acquire knowledge) in order to be able to acquire any knowledge at all.[3] The main reasons why Kant did not perceive the paradox followed from the framework in which he operated, which was the framework of the philosophy of consciousness. For Kant, the "Ich denke" (I think), the "transcendental apperception" was "that highest point to which we must ascribe all employment of the understanding, even the whole of logic, and conformally therewith, transcendental philosophy" (Kant 1929, B134).

Karl-Otto Apel's "Transformation of Philosophy"

The work of Karl-Otto Apel can be seen as a rearticulation (or transformation; see Apel, 1973; 1980) of transcendental philosophy that tries to circumvent the dogmatic element in Kant's position by making a shift from the framework of the philosophy of consciousness to that of the philosophy of language. The main difference between Kant and Apel lies in the latter's recognition of the fact that all knowledge is linguistically mediated. While Kant assumed that the acquisition of knowledge is an individualistic enterprise, Apel argues that our individual experiences must be lifted to the level of a language game in order to become knowledge. The link between experience and language is, however, not automatically established. The question of the validity of our individual experiences has to be answered by means of argumentation. Because argumentation makes sense only within a language game, within a specific "community of communication," Apel concludes that this community is the condition of possibility of all knowledge.

Apel's "linguistic turn" thus results in the recognition of the a priori of the community of communication. For Apel this community is "das Letzte, Nichthintergehbare," that is, that which cannot be surpassed (Apel quoted in Van Woudenberg, 1991: 92). Because we can never get "behind" or "before" the actual use of language in a specific community of communication, any reflection on language in formal terms can take place in and hence made possible only by a specific language game, that is, in a specific community of communication. The pragmatic dimension of language is, therefore, the most basic dimension, for which reason Apel refers to his position as "transcendental pragmatics."

Although Apel establishes a strong link between transcendental pragmatics and the really existing communities of communication—a maneuver that seems to give his project a strongly conventionalistic basis—he introduces a critical element that is meant to enable him to go beyond mere convention. This is the idea of the "ideal community of communication" or the "transcendental language game." Apel claims that a participant in a genuine argument is at the same time a member of an actual community of communication and of a counterfactual ideal community of communication, a community that is in principle open to all speakers and that excludes all force except the force of the better argument. Apel argues that any claim to intersubjectively valid knowledge implicitly acknowledges this ideal community of communication, as a meta-institution of rational argumentation, to be its ultimate source of justification (Apel, 1980: 119).

Reflexive Grounding

The idea of the ideal community of communication thus provides a criterion that makes critique possible. What distinguishes Apel's position from critical dogmatism is that this criterion is not installed dogmatically but by means of a process to which Apel refers as "reflexive grounding" ("Letztbegründung durch Reflexion"). With respect to this process, Apel claims that he can circumvent the dogmatic implications of the Münchhausen trilemma. How should this be understood?

The first thing to acknowledge is that the first and third option of the Münchausen trilemma—infinite regress and dogmatism—hang together. Both follow from the fact that Albert thinks of the process of foundation in terms of deduction. It is evident that if we talk about foundations in a deductive style, that is, if we raise the question of the "foundation of the foundation," we immediately enter an infinite regress, which can be stopped only arbitrarily. Apel admits that if we understand founding in this deductive sense, we will never find foundations. But, so he argues, this does not mean that we should give up the idea of foundation as such, but only that we need another way to bring foundations into view.

Apel's approach starts from the recognition that the conditions of possibility of argumentation have to be presupposed in all argumentation (otherwise they would not be conditions of possibility). From this it follows that one cannot argue against these conditions without immediately falling into a performative contradiction. This is the situation where the performative dimensions of the argument, that is, the act of arguing, contradicts the propositional content, that is, what is argued (like in sentences such as "I claim that I do not exist," or "I contend—thereby claiming truth—that I make no truth claim"). This implies, according to Apel, that all contentions that cannot be disclaimed without falling into a performative contradiction express a condition of the possibility of the argumentative use of language. The principle of the avoidance of the performative contradiction, in short the principle of performative consistency, thus is the criterion that can reveal the ultimate foundations of the argumentative use of language, that is, those propositions that do not need further grounding because they cannot be understood without knowing that they are true.[4]

Although Apel articulates the method and the criterion by which the ultimate foundations of the argumentative use of language can be revealed, he doesn't say much about what these foundations actually are (cf. Van Woudenberg, 1991: 134–135). Yet what the application of the principle of performative consistency can bring into view are precisely the foundations, or, as Apel calls them, the "meta-rules" of all argumentative use of language. These meta-rules—which include such things as that all communication aims at consensus; that all communication rest upon the validity of claims to truth, rightness, and truthfulness; and that these claims can in principle be redeemed—outline the ideal community of communication (see Van Woudenberg, 1991: 134–135).

Transcendental Critique

Apel's transcendental pragmatics provides an attempt to articulate the criteria for critique in a non-dogmatic way. The importance of Apel's position lies in the fact that it goes beyond the individualism of Kantian transcendental philosophy. Apel brings the transcendental approach into the realm of argumentation and communication. More than simply another conception of critique, Apel's position suggests that critical dogmatism—at least in so far as it concerns the dogmatic, or what Popper calls the irrational choice for a rational form of life—is an untenable position, because "any choice that could be understood as meaningful already presupposes the transcendental language game as its condition of possibility" (Apel, 1987a: 281). Only, therefore, "under the rational presupposition of intersubjective rules can deciding in the presence of alternatives be understood as meaningful behavior" (ibid.). From this, so Apel concludes, it does not follow that every decision is rational, but only, that a decision in favor of the principle of rational legitimation of criticism is "rational a priori" (ibid.: 282). Reason, so Apel argues, in no way needs to replace its rational justification, for "it can always confirm its own legitimation through reflection on the fact that it presupposes its own self-understanding of the very rules it opts for" (ibid.).

These remarks reveal that for Apel the criticality of transcendental critique is motivated by the principle of rationality. After all, so we could say, the "sin" of the performative contradiction is a sin against rationality. In this respect, rationality gives transcendental critique its "right" to be critical. Transcendental critique suggests a style of critique that is primarily aimed at spotting performative contradictions. It can, therefore, be understood as a specific form of internal critique, where the main critical work consists of the confrontation of a position or argument with its often implicit conditions of possibility in order to reveal whether such a position or argument is rational or not. The main advantage of the transcendental style of critique lies in the fact that it brings into vision a critical program that does not rest upon an arbitrary, dogmatic choice for criteria. In doing so, transcendental critique outlines a stronger and more consistent critical program than critical dogmatism. It will be clear, however, that the strength of transcendental critique rests upon the validity of the transcendental style of argumentation. It is at this point that I wish to turn to Derrida and deconstruction.

Deconstruction

Although in one respect Derrida's work is firmly rooted in the critical tradition that is characteristic of Western philosophy, deconstruction stands out both with respect to the *object* of its critique and with respect to its *"method."* Deconstruction is first of all special in that its critical "work" is aimed at the very possibility of critique itself. Derrida emphasizes that deconstruction is *not* a critique "in a general or Kantian sense," but that "the instance of *krinein* or of *krisis* (decision, choice, judgment, discernment) is itself ... one of the essential 'themes' or 'objects' of deconstruction" (Derrida, 1991: 273). Deconstruction, Derrida writes, "always aims at the trust confided in the critical, criticotheoretical agency, that is, the deciding agency," for which reason he concludes that "deconstruction is deconstruction of critical dogmatism" (Derrida, 1995: 54). This means that the critical "agenda" of deconstruction is first of all aimed at critical philosophy—or philosophy as critique—itself. Derrida indeed maintains that the central question of his writing is the question as to "from what site or non-site (*non-lieu*) philosophy [can] as such appear to itself as other than itself, so that it can interrogate and reflect upon itself in an original manner" (Derrida, 1984: 108).

With regard to its method—which in a sense is anything but a method (see below)—deconstruction can be understood as yet another reaction to the Münchausen trilemma. Like Apel, Derrida can be said to look for a solution along the lines of the second option of the trilemma, that is, the option of the reflexive paradox. But unlike Apel, Derrida does not try to escape the paradox by means of a transcendental "movement." He rather has chosen to stay within this paradoxical terrain in order to explore its critical potential. In doing so, Derrida has offered not only another way to think about critique and criticality but also a profound critique of the transcendental approach in that he questions the very possibility to articulate the condition of possibility in an unambiguous way.

As I have discussed in Chapter 1, the major object of Derrida's critical efforts is what he refers to as the metaphysics of presence. Derrida has aimed to put the "gesture" of the metaphysics of presence into question. But unlike Nietzsche, Freud, Heidegger and all the other "destructive discourses," Derrida has argued that we can never make a total break, that we can never step outside of the tradition that has made us. "There is no sense," he argues, "in doing without the concepts of metaphysics in order to shake metaphysics. We ... can pronounce not a single destructive proposition which has not already had to slip into the form, the logic, and the implicit postulations of precisely what it seeks to contest" (Derrida, 1978: 280). While Derrida definitely wants to "shake" metaphysics, he acknowledges that this cannot be done from some neutral and innocent place outside of metaphysics, which means that the only option left is to show the instability—and instatability—of metaphysics itself. This is why Derrida has emphasized that deconstruction is not a method "and cannot be transformed into one" (Derrida, 1991: 273), but that it rather is "one of the possible names to designate … what occurs [ce qui arrive], or cannot manage to occur [ce qui n'arrive pas à arriver], namely a certain dislocation which in effect reiterates itself regularly—and everywhere where there is something rather than nothing" (Derrida & Ewald, 1995: 287–288).

One way in which Derrida articulates the occurrence of deconstruction, as I have discussed in Chapter 1, is with the help of the "neographism" of *différance*. Derrida's discussion of *différance* takes its starting point in De Saussure's contention that language should be understood as a system of differences without positive terms. The implication of this view is that the "movement of signification" is possible only if each element "appearing on the scene of presence, is related to something other than itself" (Derrida, 1982: 13). What is called "the present" is, therefore, constituted "by means of this very relation to what it is not" (ibid.). This "contamination" is a *necessary* contamination, because for the present to be itself, it already has to be other than itself. This, as I have shown, puts the non-present in a double position, because it is the non-present that makes the presence of the present possible, and yet, it can make this presence possible only by means of its own exclusion. If this is what deconstruction can bring into view, we can already get an idea of its critical potential, because at the heart of deconstruction lies a concern for the "constitutive outside" of what presents itself as self-sufficient. This reveals that deconstruction is more than just a destruction of the metaphysics of presence. Deconstruction is first and foremost an affirmation of what is excluded and forgotten—an affirmation, in short, of what is other.

The reason why Derrida doesn't stop here but needs to introduce the neographism of *difference* is that he takes the idea of difference without positive terms to its conclusion, that is, he applies it onto itself. If it is the case, after all, that in language there are only differences without positive terms, then we have to concede that we can no longer articulate the differential character of language itself by means of a positive term, which leads to the conclusion, as we have seen, that the "play of difference," which is "the condition for the possibility and functioning of every sign, is in itself a silent play" (Derrida, 1982: 5). Strictly speaking, there is only one way to avoid this mistake, which is by acknowledging that the differences that constitute the play of difference "are themselves effects" (Derrida, 1982: 11). This means, then, that in the "most classical fashion," that is, in the language of metaphysics, we would have to speak of them as effects "without a cause" (ibid.: 12).

The predicament can be put as follows: because we are talking about the condition of possibility of all conceptuality, this condition cannot belong to what it makes possible, that is, the "order" of conceptuality. It has to be outside and come before this order. Yet the only way in which we can articulate this condition of possibility is from within this order. Because the condition of possibility is always articulated in terms of the system that is made possible by it, it is, in a sense, always already too late to be its condition of possibility. This, in turn, implies that the condition of possibility of language is at the very same time a condition of impossibility (cf. Gasché, 1986: 316–317). The impossible combination of the condition of possibility and the condition of impossibility is the central idea of Derrida's quasi-transcendentalism.

At this point, the critical potential of deconstruction returns in an even more radical way. The idea here is that because conditions of possibility are always already contaminated by the "system" that is made possible by them, this "system" is never totally delimited by these conditions. *Différance* thus expresses a quasi-transcendental or quasi-condition of possibility. As Caputo (1997: 102) puts it, *différance* does not describe fixed boundaries that delimit what can happen and what cannot "but points a mute, Buddhist finger at the moon of uncontainable effects." Deconstruction thus tries to open up the system in the name of that which cannot be thought of in terms of the system (and yet makes the system possible). This reveals that the deconstructive affirmation is not simply an affirmation of what is known to be excluded by the system. Deconstruction is an affirmation of what is wholly other, of what is unforeseeable from the present. It is an affirmation of an otherness that is always to come, as an event that "as event, exceeds calculation, rules, programs, anticipations" (Derrida, 1992: 27). Deconstruction is an openness towards the unforeseeable incoming (l'invention; invention) of the other (see Caputo, 1997: 47). It is from this concern for what is totally other, that deconstruction derives its "right" to be critical, its "right" to deconstruct—or, to be more precise, its right to reveal or witness deconstruction.

From Critique to Deconstruction

It is perhaps not too difficult to see the profound difference between deconstruction and critical dogmatism. As we have seen, "the instance of krinein or of krisis (decision, choice, judgment, discernment) is ... one of the essential "themes" or "objects" of deconstruction" (Derrida, 1991: 273), for which reason Derrida has concluded that "deconstruction is deconstruction of critical dogmatism" (Derrida, 1995: 54). Derrida has tried to show in many different ways that there is no safe ground upon which we can base our decisions, that there are no pure, uncontaminated, original criteria on which we can simply and straightforwardly base our judgments. At the basis of our decisions, as he has put it, lies a radical undecidability that cannot be closed off by our decisions but "continues to inhabit the decision" (Derrida, 1996: 87).

The distance between deconstruction and transcendental critique is perhaps less easy to grasp. Yet I wish to argue that deconstruction, although in a sense staying remarkably close to the main intuitions of transcendental pragmatics, also puts a serious challenge to this program. Apel and Derrida agree on the fact that we are always on the inside of language and history, so that the language game that made us who we are, that gives us to possibility to speak in the first place, is, in Apel's words, "nichthintergehbar" (unsurpassable). This is why Derrida has stressed that there cannot be a total rupture from the language game of metaphysics—which comes close to Apel's claim that a total critique of reason is impossible.

Difficulties arise as soon as we want to say something about what makes our speaking—and more specifically in the case of Apel, argumentation—possible. Although Apel hesitates to give a positive description of the conditions of possibility of the argumentative use of language, he at least believes that these conditions *can* be identified in a positive way by means of the principle of performative consistency. This, as I have argued, leads him eventually to the meta-rules that constitute the ideal community of communication.

Derrida is much more radical in his rejection of the possibility to identify and articulate the conditions of possibility of our speaking in any positive and unambiguous way. This is the whole point of *différance*, which is nothing less than an attempt to point at the predicament that a condition of possibility has to be "outside" of the system that is made possible by it in order for it to be a condition of possibility and yet, at the very same time, can be articulated only from the "inside" of the system that it has made possible. *Différance* is, therefore, at the very same time, inside and outside, it is both origin and effect, for which reason it can be understood only as a "quasi-condition of possibility" that—and this is crucial—does not set precise boundaries on what can happen and what cannot happen.

The crucial difference between transcendental critique and deconstruction lies precisely here. The point is that Apel has to assume that conditions of possibility control the system that is made possible by them. After all, it is only on the basis of this assumption that a performative contradiction can arise, because such a contradiction can occur only when all possible operations in the system are controlled by these conditions. What Derrida brings to the fore is that conditions of possibility can never be articulated independent of the system; they can never be articulated from some safe metaphysical position outside of the system. And it is precisely because of this that they cannot have total control over the system. What is possible, so we could say, is always more than what conditions of possibility allow for. Deconstruction wants to do justice to this unforeseeable excess.

In this respect, deconstruction can be seen as offering yet another conception of criticality (although it should by now be clear that "after" deconstruction both the idea of a conception and the idea of criticality have to be understood differently, just as the "after" of after deconstruction is not simply an after) in that it envisages another way to go beyond the present and the given, another way, in short, for judgment to become possible. Unlike critical dogmatism, this judgment does not come from some allegedly safe place "outside." Unlike transcendental critique, it doesn't come from the inside either—as a form of internal critique through a test of performative consistency. Deconstruction suggests that both resources of critique are not as pure and self-sufficient as is assumed. The critical work of deconstruction, so we could say, consists in revealing the impurity of the critical criteria, it consists in revealing that they are not self-sufficient but need something other than themselves to be(come) possible. The critical work of deconstruction, in other words, consists in "the relentless pursuit of *the* impossible, which means, of things whose possibility is sustained by their impossibility, of things which, instead of being wiped out by their impossibility, are actually nourished and fed by it" (Caputo, 1997: 32). The purpose of this is not to subvert the very possibility of critique, but rather to open up critique for its own uncritical assumptions. The aim of deconstruction—"if such a thing exists"—is not to destroy but to affirm and do justice to the impossible, to what cannot be foreseen as a possibility. This is what drives the critical work of deconstruction and it is in this sense—but only in this sense—that Derrida indeed belongs to the critical stream of Western philosophy.

Notes

1. Siegel is one of the few participants who has dealt with this issue extensively (see e.g., Siegel 1987; 1988; 1990; cf. Snik & Zevenbergen 1995, p. 112).

2. See, e.g., Orr 1989; Garrison & Phelan, 1990; Thayer-Bacon, 1992; 1993; Alston, 1995; Garrison, 1999.
3. "Die Forderung ist also diese: man soll das Erkenntnisvermögen erkennen, ehe man erkennt; es ist dasselbe wie mit dem Schwimmenwollen, ehe man ins Wasser geht. Die Untersuchung des Erkenntnisvermögens ist selbts erkennend, kann nicht zu dem kommen, zu was es kommen will, weil es selbst dies ist" (Hegel, quoted in Sas 1995: 508). Nietzsche would later express this concern quite poignantly in the following way: "(E)ine Kritiek des Erkenntnisvermögens ist unsinnig; wie sollte das Werkzeug sich selbst kritisieren können, wenn es eben nur sich zur Kritik gebrauchen kann? Es kann nicht einmal sich selbst definieren" (Nietzsche 1964, section 486).
4. In Apel's own words: "(dieses) Kriterium ... ist in der Lage, unbestreitbare Präsuppositionen der Argumentation als reflexiv-letztbegründete Sätze aufzuzeichnen: d.h., Sätze, die keiner Begründung aus etwas anderem bedürfen, weil man sie nicht verstehen kann, ohne zu wissen dass sie wahr sind" (Apel, 1987b: 185).

References

Albert, H. (1985). *Treatise on Critical Reason*. Princeton: Princeton University Press.
Alston, K. (1995). Begging the Question: Is Critical Thinking Biased? *Educational Theory* 45: 225–233.
Apel, K.-O. (1973). *Transformation der Philosophie*. Frankfurt am Main: Suhrkamp.
Apel. K.-O. (1980). *Towards a Transformation of Philosophy*. London: Routledge and Kegan Paul.
Apel, K.-O. (1987a). "The Problem of Philosophical Foundations in Light of a Transcendental Pragmatics of Language," in K. Baynes, J. Bohman, & Th. McCarthy (eds.), *After Philosophy: End or Transformation?* Cambridge, MA: MIT Press. pp. 250–290.
Apel, K.-O (1987b). "Falllibilismus, Konsenstheorie der Wahrheit und Letztbegündung," in Forum für Philosophie (eds.), *Philosphie und Begründung*. Frankfurt am Main: Suhrkamp. pp. 116–211.
Caputo, J.D. (ed.) (1997). *Deconstruction in a Nutshell. A Conversation with Jacques Derrida*. New York: Fordham University Press.
Derrida, J. (1978). *Writing and Difference*. Chicago: University of Chicago Press.
Derrida, J. (1982). *Margins of Philosophy*. Chicago: University of Chicago Press.
Derrida, J. (1984). "Deconstruction and the Other. An Interview with Jacques Derrida," in R. Kearney (ed.), *Dialogues with Contemporary Continental Thinkers*. Manchester: Manchester University Press.
Derrida, J. (1987). "Some Questions and Responses," in N. Fabb, D. Attridge, A. Durant & C. MacCabe (eds.), *The Linguistics of Writing. Arguments between Language and Literature*. Manchester, UK: Manchester University Press.
Derrida, J. (1991). "Letter to a Japanese Friend," in P. Kamuf (ed.), *A Derrida Reader: Between the Blinds*. New York: Columbia University Press. pp. 270–276.
Derrida, J. (1992a). "Force of Law: The 'Mystical Foundation of Authority,'" in D. Cornell, M. Rosenfeld & D.G. Carlson (eds.), *Deconstruction and the Possibility of Justice*. New York & London: Routledge.
Derrida, J. (1995). *Points... Interviews, 1997–1994*. Stanford, CA: Stanford University Press.

Derrida, J. (1996). "Remarks on Deconstruction and Pragmatism," in Ch. Mouffe (ed.), *Deconstruction and Pragmatism*. London & New York: Routledge. pp. 77–88.
Derrida, J. & Ewald, F. (1995). "A Certain 'Madness' Must Watch over Thinking. An Interview with Jacques Derrida," *Educational Theory* 45, 3: 273–291.
Ennis, R. (1962). "A Concept of Critical Thinking," *Harvard Educational Review* 32, 81–111.
Ennis, R. (1987). "A Taxonomy of Critical Thinking Dispositions and Abilities," in J. Baron & R. Sternberg (eds.), *Teaching for Thinking*. New York: Freeman. pp. 9–26.
Garrison, J. (1999). "Reclaiming the Lógos, Considering the Consequences, and Restoring Context," *Educational Theory* 49: 317–337.
Garrison, J. & Phelan, A. (1990). "Toward a Feminist Poetic of Critical Thinking," in R. Page (ed.), *Philosophy of Education 1989*. Normal, IL: Philosophy of Education Society.
Gasché, R. (1986). *The Tain of the Mirror: Derrida and the Philosophy of Reflection*. Cambridge, MA: Harvard University Press.
Kant, I. (1929). *Critique of Pure Reason*, N. Kemp Smith (trans.). New York: St. Martin's Press.
Kant, I. (1956). *Kritik der reinen Vernunft. Nach den ersten und zweiten Original-Ausgabe neu herausgegeben von Raymund Schmidt*. Hamburg: Felix Meiner.
Levinas, E. (1991). "Wholly Otherwise," in R. Bernasconi & S. Critchley (eds.), *Re-reading Levinas*. Bloomington, IN: Indiana University Press. pp. 3–10.
Nietzsche, F. (1964). *Der Wille zur Macht: Versuch einer Umwertung aller Werte*. Stuttgart: Alfred Kröner.
Orr, D. (1989). "Just the Facts Ma'am: Informal Logic, Gender and Pedagogy," *Informal Logic* 9: 1–10.
Peters, R. (1966). *Ethics and Education*. London: George Allen & Unwin Ltd.
Rorty, R. (1980). *Philosophy and the Mirror of Nature*. Oxford: Blackwell.
Röttgers, K. (1990). "Kritik," in J.J. Sandkühler (eds.), *Europäische Enzyklopädie zu Philosophie und Wissenschaften*. Band 2. Hamburg: Felix Meiner Verlag. pp. 889–898.
Sas, P. (1995). "Het Geweten van de Transcendentaalfilosofie: Karl-Otto Apel en de Mogelijkheid van Strikte Reflectie," *Tijdschrift voor Filosofie* 57, 505–525.
Siegel, H. (1987). *Relativism Refuted. A Critique of Contemporary Epistemological Relativsm*. Dordrecht: Reidel.
Siegel, H. (1988). *Educating Reason. Rationality, Critical Thinking and Education*. New York & London: Routledge.
Siegel, H. (1990). "Why be Rational? On Thinking Critically about Critical Thinking," in R. Page (ed.), *Philosophy of Education 1989*. Normal, IL: Philosophy of Education Society. pp. 392–401.
Snik, G.L.M. & Zevenbergen, J.K. (1995). "Kritisch Leren Denken: Posities en Problemen," *Pedagogisch Tijdschrift* 20: 101–116.
Thayer-Bacon, B. (1992). "Is Modern Critical Thinking Sexist?" *Inquiry: Critical Thinking across the Disciplines* (September), 323–340.
Thayer-Bacon, B. (1993). "Caring and Its Relationship to Critical Thinking," *Educational Theory* 43: 323–340.
Thayer-Bacon, B. (1998). Transforming and Redescribing Critical Thinking: Constructive Thinking, *Studies in Philosophy and Education* 17: 123–148.
Woudenberg, R. van (1991). Transcendentale Reflecties. Een Onderzoek naar Transcedentale Argumenten in de Contemporaine Filosofie, met Bijzondere Aandacht voor de Transcedentale Pragmatiek van Karl-Otto Apel, Vrije Universiteit, Amsterdam.

· 5 ·

EDUCATION AFTER DECONSTRUCTION: BETWEEN EVENT AND INVENTION

GERT BIESTA

Why should educators and educationalists engage with deconstruction? What could be the point of them reading the writings of Jacques Derrida? If deconstruction were just another "philosophy," then to engage with deconstruction would be an option amongst many. Some like Dewey, others prefer Wittgenstein, and still others go for Derrida. If, on the other hand, it were true that "deconstruction is the case" (Derrida, 1990: 85), that "deconstruction" "is one of the possible names to designate … what occurs [*ce qui arrive*], or cannot manage to occur [*ce qui n'arrive pas à arriver*], namely a certain dislocation which in effect reiterates itself regularly—and everywhere where there is something rather than nothing" (Derrida & Ewald, 1995: 287–288), then the relationship between deconstruction and education may well be a different one. Then the question is not about the implications of Derrida for education. Then the task is not to apply deconstruction to education. The task rather is to find out how and where deconstruction occurs or might occur in education. The task, therefore, is not to deconstruct education, but to demonstrate deconstruction in education—and perhaps also to show education-in-deconstruction (see also Bennington, 2000: 11). In this chapter, I take up this challenge by focusing on questions of subjectivity and subjectification in relation to Derrida's "inventionalism." I begin with a brief historical reconstruction not only in order to show the "position" of these questions in the modern educational tradition, but also in order to indicate why and how the question of the subject has become a problem—something that has to do with the humanist foundations of modern education. I then turn to Derrida in order to see how the way in which deconstruction occurs in education might help us to understand the invention of the other through education in a way that is able to overcome the humanist foundations of modern education.

The Opening of Modern Education

"Education" is a complicated concept. On the one hand it is used to *describe* particular practices, most often the practice of schooling; on the other hand it is used to *judge* such practices and their outcomes. However, if we wish to make judgments about educational practices, for example when asking what "good" or "effective" education is, we first have to engage with another question, which is the question of what education is *for*. A major purpose of education lies in what might be called its *qualification function*, that is, the ways in which educational practices and processes contribute to the acquisition of the knowledge, skills, and dispositions that are considered necessary to "do" something—a "doing" that can range from the very specific (such as in the case of training for a particular job) to the much more general (such as in the case of liberal education or "life skills" education). A second function of education has to do with the ways in which, through education, individuals become part of existing sociocultural, political, and moral orders. This we might call the *socialization function* of education, a function that is often understood in terms of the acquisition of norms, values, and particular ways of doing and being (which, in apolitical understandings of socialization are often depicted as the "normal" way of doing and being). Schools and other educational practices and institutions partly engage in socialization deliberately, for example, in the form of values education or character education, through attempts to turn young people into "good citizens," or when they have a role in processes of professional socialization. But socialization happens also in less visible ways, as has been made clear in the literature on the hidden curriculum and the role of schooling in the reproduction of social inequality.

Whereas some would argue that education should focus only on qualification, and whereas others defend that education has an important role to play (also) in the socialization of children and young people, there is a third "function" of education that is generally thought of as being different from qualification and socialization. This function has to do with the ways in which education contributes to the individuation or, as I prefer to call it, the *subjectification* of children and young people. The *subjectification function* might perhaps best be understood as the opposite of the socialization function. It is precisely *not* about the insertion of "newcomers" into existing orders, but about ways of being that hint at independence from such orders—ways of being in which the individual is not simply a "specimen" of a more encompassing order.

The idea of the human subject as an independent, post-traditional "center" of being and action can be traced back (at least) to the Enlightenment (see Foucault, 1984). Immanuel Kant defined Enlightenment as the release of the human being "from his [sic] self-incurred tutelage" and defined tutelage as the inability of the human being "to make use of his [sic] understanding without the direction from another" (Kant 1992[1784]: 90). This immaturity is self-incurred, according to Kant, "when its cause lies not in lack of reason but in lack of resolution and courage" (ibid.: 90). This is why he argued that human beings should have the *courage* to use their own understanding. It was the call for the courage to use one's own understanding that Kant saw as "the motto of Enlightenment" (ibid.).

From a philosophical angle, the most important aspect of Kant's conception of "rational autonomy"—autonomy based upon reason—was that he did *not* conceive of this as a contingent historical possibility, but saw it instead as something that was an inherent part of human nature. Kant described the "propensity and vocation to free thinking" as the "ultimate destination" of the human being and as the "aim of his existence" (Kant, 1982: 701; my translation). To block progress in enlightenment would, therefore, be "a crime against human nature" (Kant, 1992[1784]: 93). Interestingly enough, Kant also argued that the "propensity to free thinking" could be brought about *only* through education (see Kant, 1982: 710). Kant not only wrote that the human being "is the only creature that has to be educated" (Kant, 1982: 697; my translation); he also argued that the human being can become human—that is, a rational autonomous being—only "through education" ("Der Mensch kann nur Mensch werden durch Erziehung") (ibid.: 699).

With Kant, the rationale for education became founded upon the idea "of a certain kind of subject who has the inherent potential to become self-motivated and self-directing," while the task of education became one of bringing about or releasing this potential "so that subjects become fully autonomous and capable of exercising their individual and intentional agency" (Usher & Edwards, 1994: 24–25). Modern education thus became based upon a truth about the nature and ultimate destination of the human being, while the connection between rationality, autonomy, and education became the "Holy Trinity" of modern education. This was the case not only in approaches that emerged more or less directly from the Kantian framework, such as educational approaches based on the work of Piaget or Kohlberg. The idea of rational autonomy became a cornerstone also in critical approaches to education that took further inspiration from Hegel, Marx, and Neo-Marxism, such as the work of Freire and the Continental and North-American versions of critical pedagogy (see Biesta 1998; 2005a).

What is most significant about Kant's intervention—and this is why we can say that his work at least marks and perhaps even inaugurates the transition to modern education—is that he established a link between education and human freedom. Kant made the question of human freedom the central issue of modern education by making a distinction between heteronomous determination and self-determination and by arguing that education ultimately had to do with the latter, not the former. In a sense, therefore, that it was only after Kant that it became possible to distinguish between socialization and education and to claim that the proper interest of education is an interest in subjectification. In Kantian terms, this is an interest in bringing about autonomy, emancipation, and freedom.

The Closure of Modern Education

Whereas, on the one hand, Kant opened up a whole new realm for educational thought and practice—and the idea that education should bring about rational autonomy has remained central to many educational theories and practices up to the present day (see, e.g., Winch, 2005)—on the other hand, he closed off this opening almost before it could start. This happened along two, related lines. It was first of all because Kant allowed for only *one* definition of what it meant to be human. With Kant "rational autonomy" became the marker of humanity, which left those who were considered to be not or not-yet rational—including children—in a difficult position. It was also because for Kant rational autonomy was *not* understood as a contingent historical possibility, but as a necessity firmly rooted in the nature of the human being so that education thus became founded upon a particular *truth* about the nature and destiny of the human being. (A further effect of this is that education became strongly connected with questions about psychological development.)

For a long time, the closure entailed in the Kantian articulation of the foundations of modern education went unnoticed. This was partly because there was widespread support for the underlying belief that human beings are ultimately rational beings who strive for autonomy. This, after all, was very much the "agenda" of the French, German, and Scottish Enlightenment. Yet, and more importantly, the closure in Kant's articulation of the foundations of modern education went unnoticed also because those who were excluded by this definition of the human being—those who were deemed to be irrational or pre-rational (such as children)—lacked a voice to protest against their own exclusion, and they lacked this voice precisely because of the particular definition of what it meant to be human. They were excluded, in other words, before they could even speak or before they could even be acknowledged as capable of speaking (see also Rancière, 1995; Biesta, 2007).

Whereas Kant thought that he had moved education away from tradition and socialization towards autonomy and freedom, we now live in a world in which the Kantian idea of rational autonomy has been moved back from the "side" of freedom to the "side" of tradition. There are not only important philosophical reasons why we should see rational autonomy as a contingent historical achievement rather than as a natural necessity or as the *telos* of history. I wish to claim that many of the most problematic clashes between different cultures and traditions[1] in our time center precisely on the question of whether the modern, Western worldview is itself "beyond" tradition or whether it should be seen as just one tradition amongst many. If we take the latter view—and I have argued elsewhere that there are compelling reasons for doing so (see particularly Biesta, 2006)—it means, educationally speaking, that modern education becomes one more form of socialization, namely, socialization into a (or as some would argue, *the*) rational form of life. This does not automatically disqualify this particular form of life, but it does make clear that a choice for such a trajectory is indeed a *choice*—a choice that has to be made by someone—and not something that is self-evident or a natural necessity.

Philosophically one way of exposing what is problematic about the way in which the modern educational project was inaugurated is by focusing on its humanist foundations. I use "humanism" here in the philosophical sense of the word, that is, as the idea that it is possible to know and express the essence or nature of the human, and also that it is possible to use this knowledge as the foundation for subsequent action—not only in the sphere of education but also, for example, in the sphere of politics. Humanism, as Emmanuel Levinas has put it, entails "the recognition of an invariable essence named 'Man,' the affirmation of his central place in the economy of the Real and of his value which [engenders] all values" (Levinas, 1990: 227). Modern education in its Kantian form is clearly humanistic since it is founded upon a particular *truth* about the nature of the human being.

In twentieth-century philosophy, humanism has basically been challenged for two reasons. On the one hand, questions have been raised about the *possibility* of humanism, that is, about the possibility for human beings to define their own essence and origin. Here we can think of the work of Foucault and Derrida who both have exposed the impossibility of capturing the essence and origin of the human—an impossibility that has become known as the "death of the subject" (see Foucault 1970; see also Derrida, 1982). On the other hand questions have been raised about the *desirability* of humanism. This line has particularly been developed by Heidegger and Levinas (see Biesta, 2006 for more detail; see also Derrida, 1982: 109–136). For Levinas the "crisis of humanism in our society" began with the "inhuman events of recent history" (Levinas, 1990: 279). Yet for Levinas the crisis of humanism is not simply located in these inhumanities as such, but first and foremost in humanism's inability to effectively counter such inhumanities and also in the fact that many of the inhumanities of the twentieth century—"[t]he 1914 War, the Russian Revolution refuting itself in Stalinism, fascism, Hitlerism, the 1939–45 War, atomic bombings, genocide and uninterrupted war" (ibid.)—were actually based upon and motivated by particular definitions of what it means to be human. This is why Levinas concludes—with a phrase reminiscent of Heidegger—that "[h]umanism has to be denounced ... because it is not *sufficiently* human" (Levinas, 1981: 128; emphasis added).

The problem with humanism, so we might say, is that it posits a *norm* of "humaneness," a norm of what it means to be human, and in doing so excludes all those who do not live up to or are unable to live up to this norm. At the dawn of the twenty-first century, we know all too well that this is not simply a theoretical possibility. Many of the atrocities that have become the markers of the twentieth century—such as the holocaust and the genocides in Cambodia, Rwanda, and Bosnia—were actually based upon a definition of what counts as and, more importantly, of *who* counts as human.

From an educational point of view, the problem with humanism is that it specifies a norm of what it means to be human *before* the actual manifestation of "instances" of humanity. Humanism specifies what the child, student, or newcomer *must* become, before giving them an opportunity to show who they are and who they will be. Humanism thus seems to be unable to be open to the possibility that newcomers might radically alter our understandings of what it means to be human. This means that at a fundamental level humanism can indeed think of education only as socialization because it is unable to grasp the uniqueness of each individual human being. It can think of each "newcomer" only as an instance of a human essence that has already been specified and is already known in advance.

As long as we see education through the lens of socialization, all this is, of course, not really a problem. Yet it is here that Kant remains important because he has left us with the idea that it might be—and in a sense *ought to be*—possible to make a meaningful distinction between education and socialization. If we are committed to this distinction, if we are committed to what Foucault has so aptly referred to as Enlightenment's "undefined work of freedom" (Foucault, 1984: 46), then it becomes important to think again about the ways in which we might be able to distinguish education from socialization, both in theory and in practice, and to do so in a way that does not bring us back to humanism.

Derrida's Inventionalism

As has been made clear in the previous chapters, Derrida has never operated on the side of those who have wanted to do away with the subject—and as a matter of fact most if not all of those who have been engaged in discussions about the "death of the subject" and "the end of man" have not argued against the human subject (if such an argument would be meaningful in the first place), but against the humanistic definition of human subjectivity, that is, against attempts to "fix" and "pin down" the human subject. For Derrida "(t)he ontological questioning that deals with the *subjectum*, in its Cartesian and post-Cartesian forms, is anything but a liquidation" (Derrida, 1995: 257).

As I have argued in Chapter 1, the very "thing" that drives and motivates deconstruction—or to be more precise, the very thing that drives and motivates Derrida's continuous attempts to show metaphysics-in-deconstruction—is justice (after all, for Derrida deconstruction is justice). Yet for Derrida justice is not some abstract concept that hovers above everything we do. Following Levinas, whose definition of justice is one that according to Derrida "is very minimal but which I love," Derrida defines justice as "the relation to the other" and "(t)hat is all" (Derrida, 1997: 17). If justice is a "concern" for the other as other, for the otherness of the other, for an otherness that, by definition, we can neither foresee nor totalize, if justice, in short, always addresses itself to the singularity of the other (Derrida, 1992a: 20), we are obliged—in the very name of justice—to keep the unforeseen possibility of the in-coming of the other, the surprise of the "invention" of the other, open (see Derrida, 1989). The other, after all, is "precisely what is not invented" (Derrida, 1989: 59–60).

Derrida's "inventionalism" is, therefore, not about me inventing the other, but about the invention, the in-coming of the other, which is why "deconstructive inventiveness can consist only in opening, in unclosetting, destabilizing foreclosionary structures so as to allow for the passage toward the other" (ibid.). This is why Derrida's "inventionalism" is important for education—and more importantly for education after the "death of the subject"—because it approaches the question of human subjectivity in a radically open manner, as something that intervenes, that comes from the "outside," that comes in and breaks through our expectations and conceptions. The invention of the other has to be approached as something that is fundamentally incalculable; it is not something that can be produced, programmed, guaranteed, or even predicted. An invention "has to declare itself to be the invention of that which did not appear to be possible; otherwise it only makes explicit a program of possibilities within the economy of the same" (Derrida, 1989: 60). That is why "inventionalism" can help us to maintain a distinction between socialization and subjectification as it understands the question of subjectification—the question of the singularity of the subject, as Derrida would say—as something that breaks through the "order" of socialization, the order of the present and the same.

But how and where might this "take place" in education? How and where does deconstruction "occur" in education and how might the occurrence of deconstruction be connected with the in-coming of the other? I wish to look at two aspects of education: the relationship between teaching and learning and the curriculum. In both cases I wish to highlight the way in which a deconstructive "logic" is at stake, that is, a "logic" where conditions of possibility are "crossed" by conditions of impossibility in a way in which what is made possible is not wiped out by its impossibility but actually "nourished and fed by it" (Caputo, 1997: 32) and where the central concern is about an education that allows for the invention of the other.

Teaching and Learning: Mind the Gap!

Although a lot has been said about the problems of a transmission view of education—and I would agree that the transmission metaphor is inadequate for understanding how teaching impacts on learning—there can be no doubt that transmission is an important *aim* of educational processes and practices and that, in a certain sense (but see below), transmission is, therefore, an adequate *description* of certain (successful) educational practices. The aim of driving lessons is, after all, for the one taking the lessons to acquire the knowledge, skills, and understanding to be able to drive a car safely, just as the education of brain surgeons is aimed at the acquisition of the knowledge, skills, and understanding to conduct brain surgery in an effective and successful manner. This is why education should not be confused with learning (see also Biesta 2005b; Osberg & Biesta, 2008), since education is always bounded by a certain "teleology," that is, by an intention for a particular kind of learning to take place. Not any learning will count as successful.

But when we ask how we can understand and explain the interaction between teaching and learning and the impact of teaching on learning, a different picture emerges. Whereas teachers might wish to be able to transmit knowledge or skills to their students—and while students might wish that such knowledge and skills would simply flow into them as a result of the activities of the teacher—the point is that if teaching is going to have any effect at all upon students it is first of all because of the activities and interpretations of the students. In this respect, there is no difference between education and communication more generally: communication does not simply depend on the activities of the "sender" but also on the interpretations on the side of the "receiver" (who, for that very reason, is more than just a receiver). Because of this, as I have already alluded to in Chapter 1, all communication runs the risk of misunderstanding. But what is the position of misunderstanding in communication? One of the places where Derrida deals with this issue is in a discussion of Austin's speech act theory (see Derrida, 1988).

Derrida observes that while Austin acknowledges the fact that (performative) speech acts always run the risk of misunderstanding, he nevertheless tries to exclude this risk as something that is accidental and exterior to "normal" communication. Austin's strategy for this is to define necessary conditions for successful communication (see Derrida, 1988: 14–15). Contrary to Austin, Derrida suggests that if the failure of speech acts is a general risk, that is, if it is *always* possible that speech acts are misunderstood, then the question should be raised whether this "necessary possibility" of failure might not better be understood as constitutive of, and not—as Austin does—as an exception to "normal" communication (ibid.: 15).

The reason why Derrida argues that misunderstanding should be seen as constitutive of understanding lies in the observation that a speech act that is *not* misunderstood can exist only if the context in which such a speech act disseminates is *exhaustively* determined, that is, if there is total control over the way in which this speech act is taken up by others (see ibid.: 18). Such an exhaustive determination can, however, never be an empirical reality because, as we have seen, every speech act, every utterance needs to be interpreted by others in order to be meaningful and convey meaning. The dissemination of speech acts is, therefore, inherently unpredictable. This, in turn, means, according to Derrida, that the idea of the exhaustive determination of the context of dissemination is an "idealized image," an "ethical and teleological determination" of this context (ibid.: 17)—not an empirical reality. The general risk or failure, therefore, doesn't surround language "like a kind of *ditch* or external place of perdition which speech...can escape by remaining 'at home,' by and in itself." On the contrary, this risk is "its internal and positive condition of possibility" (ibid.).

The plausibility of Derrida's argument becomes clear when we imagine a situation in which language would be without risk. In such a situation, communication—and social interaction more generally—would have ceased to be what Derrida refers to as an *event*. Instead it would have become a strictly mechanical, a strictly calculable and predictable process. Under such conditions, it would actually be meaningless to intervene in social interaction by means of speech acts. In such a mechanistic universe, an utterance such as "I promise" would add nothing to the interaction, because all the possible consequences of any action would already be determined and would already be strictly transparent for all other actors, whose own reactions would already be determined as well. The fact that speech acts can always and structurally fail, therefore, suggests that human interaction and human communication are *not* mechanistic—they are *events*.

Derrida's account implies several things. It first of all highlights the deconstructive "nature" of education, that is, the fact that the successful transmission of knowledge or skills from teacher to student depends upon the interpretations by students of what is being taught—interpretations that are never determined by the teaching and, therefore, always contain the risk of misunderstanding and misinterpretation. This shows that the very condition of possibility of successful education is also its condition of impossibility. The most important thing about Derrida's argument is, however, not simply the fact that communication relies on interpretation and, therefore, can always go "wrong." It rather lies in his insight that if communication would go "right"—that is, if the context in which a speech act disseminates is totally determined—then there would no longer be a possibility for the invention, for the in-coming of the other (which also implies that what Austin sees as the beginning of communication is actually its end). If we take away the risk involved in communication—and perhaps Derrida would add, if we were able to take away the risk involved in communication—we also take away the opportunity for the in-coming of the other as other. Derrida's insistence on the necessary role of misunderstanding should, therefore, be read not as a plea for a release from the rules and constraints and interpretation and understanding—a kind of "hermeneutics free-for-all" (Norris, 1987: 139)—but as motivated by a concern for the impossible possibility of the in-coming of the other.

The radical indeterminacy of the interaction between teaching and learning does not mean that there is no connection between the two at all, or that any connection is only a matter of sheer luck. On the contrary, in the day-to-day practice of schooling we see many examples of "successful" teaching. The point is, however, that these are not the result of some mysterious "quality" of "effective" teachers but are rather brought about by processes that sanction and approve of *some* responses and interpretations of students and not of others. The gap between teaching and learning is closed, in other words, through processes of assessment. Assessment is, however, a highly normative activity since it brings in judgments about success and failure, about desirable and undesirable interpretations on the side of students. This is why in those cases in which assessment creates a close connection—and perhaps we might say a closed connection—between teaching and learning, this is not the result of the successful transmission of knowledge and skills from teacher to student, but rather the effect of a particular normative intervention in- and perhaps we should call this a normative closure of—the ways in which students respond to and make sense of what they are being taught. Such "success" is, in other words, an "idealized image" and an "ethical and teleological determination" (ibid.: 17). Once we can see deconstruction in education, we can begin to grasp that assessment sanctions not only particular "outcomes" in terms of the qualification function of education but also particular ways of being and doing and thus also impacts upon the socialization and subjectification function of education. As long as the gap between teaching and learning is allowed to exist, there is at least the opportunity for the impossible possibility of the in-coming of the other—of the coming into the world of new beginnings and new beginners, as I have termed it elsewhere (Biesta, 2006). Any attempt to close this gap, to deny the deconstructive nature of education, therefore, threatens this possibility and thus brings subjectification back to socialization, to the insertion of the other, the newcomer, into the order or "economy" of the present and the same.

Curriculum, Representation, and the Pedagogy of Invention

Whereas the question of the relationship between teaching and learning focuses on how particular "content" can be transmitted from the student to the teacher, Derrida also helps us to raise questions about the status of content—and thus of the curriculum more generally. This is the issue of educational presentation and in this section I briefly discuss Gregory Ulmer's intriguing exploration of the role of presentation and representation in teaching (see Ulmer, 1985).

Ulmer argues that educational presentation— that is, the presentation in education of knowledge, understanding, values, the curriculum, etcetera—has traditionally been understood in terms of *re*presentation: teaching as the act of representing the world outside of the classroom. In this approach, the teacher is supposed to be a "faithful transmitter" of some original "presence" that either precedes the act of teaching or is anticipated by it. The main problem with this understanding of the process of education is that there cannot be a totally faithful transmission because "simply stated—every pedagogical exposition, just like every reading, adds something to what it transmits" (Ulmer, 1985: 162). As Derrida has put it, it is an illusion to think that one can look at a text without touching it, "without laying a hand on the 'object,' without risking—which is the only chance of entering into the game, by getting a few fingers caught—the addition of some new thread" (Derrida, 1981: 63).

The traditional way to escape this predicament has been to replace *re*presentation by presentation. This is, for example, the strategy followed by many progressive educators who tried to bring "real life" into the classroom in order to overcome the "verbalism" and the artificial nature of educational representation. It can also be seen in many contemporary attempts to allow children and young people to "learn from life," rather than from schooling. The idea behind such approaches is to let the world speak for itself, "in its own words, in its own voice, in its own logos" (Derrida, 1981: 31).

However, the assumption that the world can simply be present and can simply be presented, the assumption that we would be able to go back to the world "as it is" in and for itself, in its own original presence, is a problematic assumption. This is not only because the world never speaks for itself but always requires *our* descriptions. It is also because there is no original consciousness, no pre-linguistic and pre-social center of perception and experience to which the world is simply present. We need to engage children *in* a "form of life" and a "language game" before we can begin to speak meaningfully with them *about* the world.

This shows that the traditional idea of teaching as representation and the "progressive" idea of teaching as presentation *both* bear the traces of the metaphysics of presence. They both operate on the assumption that the full, immediate presence of "the world" is possible, either as something that "governs" and "warrants" the educational representations or as that with which children and students can and should be confronted directly. What is made invisible in both cases is that the world does not speak and cannot speak for itself, that the world can never be simply present and comprehensible in its immediacy. Yet both the strategy of representation and the strategy of presentation try to pretend that the activities of the teacher and the influence of the school-context is neutral, accidental, and effaceable. This is what lies behind the assumption that teaching, as Ulmer calls it, can be an act of "faithful transmission." It is also what lies behind the assumption that it would be possible to present life as it is in the classroom.

Ulmer argues that the construction of the scene of teaching as faithful transmission precisely creates the illusion of a presence outside of the scene of teaching that fixes, defines, and secures the meaning—if not the truth—of what is (re)presented in the classroom. The originality of what is presented or represented in education is, in other words, the *result* of the ways in which the scene of teaching is constructed. Yet it is precisely this construction of the scene of teaching that encourages "the undesirable pedagogical effect of discipleship" (Ulmer, 1985: 173). It is for this reason that Ulmer argues that we need a "new pedagogy" that must attempt to do away with this effect, since "the least thoughtful relationship to knowledge is discipleship" (ibid.).

The crucial question is what such a new pedagogy might look like. How can teachers and educators question the metaphysics of presence that underlies traditional pedagogy, and how can they do this in the very "act" of their teaching? For Ulmer, the solution to this is not to be found in a *non*-representational pedagogy but rather in a pedagogy that is *more* representational than the traditional pedagogy of representation. This is a pedagogy that does not attempt to hide away the fact that any construction of the scene of teaching, any attempt to bring the world into the classroom, either under the heading of "representation" or under the heading of (progressivist) "presentation," always entails inscription, translation, and transformation. It is a pedagogy that at the very same time makes clear that what is presented in education is not the translation or transformation of something that is more original than the translation itself. It is a pedagogy that highlights what Derrida has called *originary translation*—"if this absurd expression may be risked" (Derrida, 1978: 237). It is a pedagogy in which, as Ulmer puts it, there is "a systematic foregrounding of the pedagogic effect itself" (Ulmer, 1985: 183).

What makes all this difficult is that the "pedagogic effect" cannot be articulated in a positive way. It cannot simply be presented. It is not that teachers can simply say that what is being taught is *not* how things really are. It is also not that teachers can simply say that the world to which their representations refer is not how the world "really" in and for itself is—not in the least because the way in which the world is represented in the classroom is precisely how the world really is. What Ulmer is suggesting, therefore, is not the same as saying that everything is a social construction, that it all depends on one's own perspective. It rather is a systematic attempt to foreground the *undecidibility* at stake in presence and representation. It is to foreground that just as presence is the condition of possibility of representation, representation is the condition of possibility of presence—which means that it is also its condition of *im*possibility.

In terms of pedagogy, Ulmer has suggested a "gramatological classroom" in which teaching and learning are organized around the principle of the "hieroglyph" (ibid.: 265), which he understands as an "ideogrammatic/pictorial form" of writing that provokes a response from the "receiver," a response that is not only rational but also physiological and subconscious (see ibid.). This idea draws on the notion, well developed in psychoanalysis, that the consciousness is affected *before* any meaning is formed. It is only through an *addition to itself* (the response of the "receiver"), Ulmer argues, that the hieroglyph becomes "receivable." Without such a response, it is "unreceivable" (i.e., not understandable in itself). Because every presentation of a hieroglyph provokes a subjective response (a text) that adds itself to the presented text, every such presentation must be understood as bringing forth a wider reading of itself. It combined subjective and presented elements into something different (a "double text"). A grammatological pedagogy, so Ulmer claims, is, therefore, fundamentally inventionalistic. It takes into account an emergentist mode of meaning-making (see also Osberg & Biesta, 2008), which is neither "inner speech" nor "objective writing" but an elaboration of both that always brings something new into the world (see Ulmer, 1985: 157–188). What is taking place in the grammatological classroom, therefore, is not the reproduction of existing meaning. What is taking place is *"inventio"* (ibid.: xii).

Ulmer considered the presentational strategies adopted by the German performance artists Joseph Beuys (1921–1986) to be exemplary in illustrating how a grammatological pedagogy might actually be performed. Beuys produced many stand-alone works, but during his lifetime he would present "explanations" of his art that were an integral part of the artworks themselves. According to Ulmer's interpretation, these presentations were designed to stimulate the audience to produce something in response to the performance (see ibid.: 251). What Ulmer tries to put across is that these performances were not aimed at *transferring* a message,[2] but that they were designed to "move" the spectator into producing a message. The message was produced as memories were explored, "not to recover the past but … in order to think with them in the future" (ibid.: 240). According to Ulmer, the evocative nature of Beuys's presentations generated rather than transmitted meaning. For Ulmer meaning "comes through" already contaminated by other layers of meaning. The effect is the genesis of something new—and *inventio*.

Conclusions: Education between Event and Invention

My conclusions will be brief. In this chapter, I have indicated how the question of the subject became a central question for modern education. I have also shown how the humanistic definition of the subject that initially opened up education to the question of subjectification closed off this opening almost before it could start—although it took a long time before this closing was perceived and appreciated. I have introduced Derrida's inventionalism as a response to the problem of humanism and have shown how the occurrence of deconstruction in education—in teaching and learning, in pedagogy and curriculum—has the potential for the impossible possibility of the in-coming of the other. Much depends, however, on whether we as educators are able to live with the risk involved in approaching education as an *event*—whether we allow for deconstruction to occur in education so that the event of the in-coming of the other might happen. It is, after all, only under these impossible conditions that a meaningful distinction between education and socialization can (again) be made.

Notes

1. I speak in a general sense about cultures and traditions, because I do not want to single out particular traditions as more "traditional" than others. This is why I do not refer to, for example, religious traditions because although they figure prominently in many "clashes" that

characterize the times we live in, I do believe that, for example, the "Western" or "secular" or "scientific" traditions are as traditional as the religious tradition is. This is not to suggest that they are all the same, either in their intentions or their effects. The only thing I do not want to claim is that there is a natural ranking order of traditions.

2. Perhaps one of Beuys's most famous performances/explanations was "How to Explain Pictures to a Dead Hare," which he performed for the first time in 1965. See http://www.beuys.org/. The dead hare can be understood as symbolizing the impossibility to simply explain pictures, the impossibility of simply transferring a message.

References

Bennington, G. (2000) *Interrupting Derrida*. London and New York: Routledge.

Biesta, G.J.J. (1998) "Say You Want a Revolution..." Suggestions for the impossible future of critical pedagogy. *Educational Theory* 48(4), 499–510.

Biesta, G.J.J. (2005a) "What Can Critical Pedagogy Learn from Postmodernism? Further Reflections on the Impossible Future of Critical Pedagogy," in Ilan Gur Ze'ev (ed.), *Critical Theory and Critical Pedagogy Today. Toward a New Critical Language in Education*. Haifa: Studies in Education (University of Haifa). pp. 143–159.

Biesta, G.J.J. (2005b) Against Learning. Reclaiming a Language for Education in an Age of Learning. *Nordisk Pedagogik* 25(1), 54–66.

Biesta, G.J.J. (2006) *Beyond Learning: Democratic Education for a Human Future*. Boulder, CO: Paradigm Publishers.

Biesta, G.J.J. (2007) "Don't Count Me In." Democracy, Education and the Question of Inclusion. *Nordisk Pedagogik* 27(1), 18–31.

Derrida, J. (1978) *Writing and Difference*. Chicago: University of Chicago Press.

Derrida, J. (1981) *Dissemination*. Chicago: University of Chicago Press.

Derrida, J. (1982) *Margins of Philosophy*. Chicago: Chicago University Press.

Derrida, J. (1988) *Limited Inc*. Evanston, IL: Northwestern University Press.

Derrida, J. (1989) "Psyche: Inventions of the Other," in L.L. & W. Godzich (eds.), *Reading de Man Reading*. Minneapolis: University of Minnesota Press.

Derrida, J. (1990) "Some Statements about Truisms and Neologisms, Newisms, Postisms, Parasitisms, and Other Small Seismisms," in D. Carroll (ed.), *The States of "Theory," History, Art, and Critical Discourse*. New York: Columbia University Press.

Derrida, J. (1995) *Points... Interviews, 1994*. Stanford CA: Stanford University Press.

Derrida, J. (1997) "The Villanova Roundtable: A Conversation with Jacques Derrida," in J.D. Caputo (ed.), *Deconstruction in a Nutshell. A Conversation with Jacques Derrida*. New York: Fordham University Press.

Derrida, J. & Ewald, F. (1995) "A Certain 'Madness' Must Watch over Thinking. An Interview with Jacques Derrida," *Educational Theory* 45.3: 273–291.

Foucault, M. (1970) *The Order of Things. An Archeology of the Human Sciences*. New York: Random House.

Foucault, M. (1984) "What is Enlightenment?" in P. Rabinow (ed.), *The Foucault reader*. New York: Pantheon Books. pp. 32–50.

Kant, Immanuel (1982) "Über Pädagogik," in I. Kant, *Schiften zur Anthropologie, Geschichtsphilosophie, Politik und Pädagogik*. Frankfurt am Main: Insel Verlag. pp. 695–761.

Kant, I. (1992[1784]) An Answer to the Question "What Is Enlightenment?" in P. Waugh (ed.), *Post-modernism: A Reader*. London: Edward Arnold. pp. 89–95.
Levinas, E. (1981) *Otherwise than Being or Beyond Essence*. The Hague: Martinus Nijhoff.
Levinas, E. (1990) *Difficult Freedom. Essays on Judaism*. Baltimore: Johns Hopkins University Press.
Norris, C. (1987) *Derrida*. Cambridge, MA: Harvard University Press.
Osberg, D.C. & Biesta, G.J.J. (2008) The Emergent Curriculum: Navigating a Complex Course between Unguided Learning and Planned Enculturation. *Journal of Curriculum Studies 40(3)*, 313–328.
Rancière, J.s (1995) *La mésentente*. Paris: Gallilée.
Ulmer, G. (1985) *Applied Grammatology. Post(e)-Pedagogy from Jacques Derrida to Joseph Beuys*. Baltimore and London: Johns Hopkins University Press.
Usher, R. & Edwards, R. (1994) *Postmodernism and Education*. London/New York: Routledge.
Winch, C. (2005) *Education, Autonomy and Critical Thinking*. London/New York: Routledge.

· 6 ·

THE UNIVERSITY AND THE FUTURE OF THE HUMANITIES

MICHAEL A. PETERS

Introduction: Philosophy of the University after Nietzsche

In the essay "Expeditions of an Untimely Man" from *Twilight of the Idols,* Nietzsche writes a section entitled "*Criticism of Modernity*" beginning with the words:

> Our institutions are no longer fit for anything: everyone is unanimous about that. But the fault lies not with them but in *us*. Having lost all instincts out of which institutions grow, we are losing the institutions themselves, because *we* are no longer fit for them.... For institutions to exist there must exist the kind of will, instinct, imperative which is anti-liberal to the point of malice: the will to tradition, to authority, to centuries-long responsibility, to *solidarity* between succeeding generations backwards and forwards *in infinitum*... The entire West has lost those instincts out of which institutions grow, out of which the future grows: perhaps nothing goes so much against the grain of its "modern" spirit as this. One lives for today, one lives very fast—one lives very irresponsibly: it is precisely this one calls "freedom." (1968; orig. 1888: 93–94)

In passages such as the one above in *Twilight of the Idols*, and in *Beyond Good and Evil* and *The Will to Power,* Nietzsche identifies the break with tradition as the defining feature of modernity and underscores its accompanying recognition that the sources of its values can no longer be based upon appeals to the authority of the past. Modernity understood as a break with the past—an aesthetic, political, and epistemological break—encourages a self-consciousness of the present and an orientation to the future based on notions of change, progress, experiment, innovation, and newness. Most importantly, modernity involves that myth it constructs about itself that it is able to create its own values and normative orientations somehow out of its own historical force, movement, and trajectory. Nietzsche rejects any simple-minded opposition and refuses to embrace one option or the other unreservedly; rather, we might see him contemplating how and why "we moderns" want to draw up the historical stakes in terms of such an exhaustive dichotomy (see Peters, 2000).

Mindful of Nietzsche's critique of modernity, post-Nietzschean philosophy of the university develops along two interrelated lines. The first, pursued by Weber and continued by Heidegger, Jaspers, Lyotard, and Bourdieu, emphasizes the dangers of economic interest vested in the university through the dominance of technical reason. The second, initiated by members of the Frankfurt School and developed differently by Foucault, traces the imprint and controlling influence of the state in the academy through the apparatus of administrative reason. Jacques Derrida (2001), in novel and unexpected ways, has contributed to both lines of inquiry. He has done something different by engaging in a deconstructive analysis that is both affirmative and utopian. He has pointed to the university to come and the future of the professions within a place of resistance and yet maintained the historical link to two ideas that mediate and condition both the humanities and the performative structure of acts of profession: human rights and crimes against humanity. Derrida (2001) maintains that the "modern university should be unconditional," by which he means that it should have the "freedom" to assert, to question, to profess, and to "say everything" in the manner of a literary fiction. In this chapter, first, I discuss what Derrida calls "the future of the profession or the university without conditions." Second, I pick up on a series of criticisms raised by Richard Rorty against Derrida's concept of literature and his status as a "private ironist." Third, I examine Derrida in relation to the ends of literature and the university, under the impact of globalization and new technologies of communication. Finally, in a postscript, I return to the university and its postcolonial possibilities.

The Future of the Profession or the University without Conditions

The unconditionality of the university *without conditions* is deemed to have close links to the "humanities" to the extent that it relates to two historical ideas:

the rights of man (human rights), and crimes against humanity. The university without conditions does not exist, but it presupposes a place of critical resistance, a form of dissidence. This is its strength and also its vulnerability, what enables it to be bypassed or recuperated by instance of power.

Within the university, professors profess, perform acts of profession. Derrida relates profession to confession in terms of the general structure of any performative—promising, witnessing, etcetera—and in order to relate professing to an act of faith, which in turn relates to the structure of literary fiction that takes the form of a performative than a constative set of utterances, as well as to what he calls a "politics of the virtual." He also alludes to the proliferation of forms of confession currently evident in public and private discourse.

The performative gesture of professing is described in terms of an "as if" by means of the fragment: "As if the end of work were the beginning of the world." This is analyzed in terms of (1) a fantasy; (2) via Kant's Third Critique and the "reflective judgment" which he calls "an agent of deconstructive ferment" although it is inscribed within an opposition between nature and freedom that he has analyzed and critiqued in a number of texts; (3) the humanities as a site of the analysis and perhaps production of performative "works"—*oeurves*— rather than just work (*travail*), which remains related to a type of expiation (before the fall there was no work; at the end there will no longer be work, etc.). There is some discussion on the types of labor, distinctions between professing and a trade or using a craft, and of Jeremy Rifkin's (1995) *The End of Work: The Decline of the Global Labour Force* and the dawn of the post-market era, with which he disagrees for failing to acknowledge the enormous disparity between different countries, economies, etcetera, in terms of the so-called third technological revolution, and Jacques Le Goff's (1991) *Un autre Moyen Age*. Obviously something serious is happening to what we call work, by means of the techno-scientific mutation and by means of globalization, what he refers to throughout as "worldization" (*modialization*).

The task of the humanities to come would be

> ad infinitum, to know and to think their own history in at least the directions that can be seen to open up (the act of professing, the theology and history of work, knowledge and of faith in knowledge, the question of man, of the world, of fiction, of the performative and the "as if", of literature and of the oeuvre, etc...). (Derrida, 2001: 240)

He advances seven programmatic (and telegrammatic) tasks for the Humanities, which, because of their richness in conception and power to revitalize the humanities, require some short explanation and brief elaboration.

1. These new Humanities would treat the history of man, the idea, the figure, and the notion of "what is proper to man" (and a non-finite series of oppositions by which man is determined, in particular the traditional opposition of the life-form called human and of the life-form called animal). (Derrida, 2001: 241).

Derrida treats the history of man via the rights of man (and women) and the concept of crimes against humanity. Both concepts he treats as juridical performatives; and he historicizes them—the first, "transformed and enriched" during the period 1789 to 1948, the second, mapping the "geopolitical field of international law" since the end of World War II.

2. These new Humanities would treat, in the same style, the history of democracy and the idea of sovereignty, that is to say as well, of course, the conditions or rather the unconditionality on which the university and within it the Humanities are supposed (once again the "as if") to live. (Derrida, 2001: 242)

Thus, as Derrida elaborates, the deconstruction of the concept of sovereignty would encompass questions of international law, the limits of the nation-state, and the way the notion of sovereignty impinges upon juridical-political discourses governing the relations between man and woman.

3. These new Humanities would treat, in the same style, the history of "professing", of the "profession", and the professoriat, a history articulated with that of the premises or presuppositions (notably Abrahamic, biblical, and above all Christian) of work and of the worldwide-ised confession. (Derrida, 2001: 243)

The profession, he adds, both in relation to and in a way that goes beyond the question of sovereignty, the nation-state, the 'people' and even democracy. Derrida also talks here of the 'immense problem' of dissociating democracy from citizenship.

4. These Humanities would treat, in the same style, the history of literature. (Derrida, 2001: 243)

That is, literature, its canons, the history of the concept of literature and its links to fiction and the performative "as if", and concepts of oeuvre, author, signature, and national language. Derrida singles out "the right to say or not to say everything that founds both democracy" and the university.

5. These Humanities would treat, in the same style, the history of professing, the profession of faith, professionalisation, and professoriat. (Derrida, 2001: 243)

The question here is whether we are "witnessing the end of a certain figure of the professor and of his or her supposed authority".

> 6. These Humanities would thus finally treat, in the same style...the history of the "as if" and especially the history of this precious distinction between performative acts and constative acts. (Derrida, 2001: 244)

Derrida addresses himself to not only the distinction but also to the history of this distinction beginning with Austin's "brilliant oeuvre", and its inheritance. Finally, he arrives at the seventh point; as he says in an earlier version, "Note a sabbatical!"

> 7. Or rather I let perhaps arrive at the end, now, the very thing that, by arriving, by taking place or having place, revolutionizes, overturns, and puts to rout the ver authority that is attached, in the university, in the Humanities:
>
>   (i) to knowledge (or at least to its model of constative language);
>
>   (ii) to the profession or to the profession of faith (or at least to its model of performative language);
>
>   (iii) to the mise en oeuvre, the putting to work, at least to the performative putting to work of the "as if". (Derrida, 2001: 244).

The fecundity of Derrida's approach is to link a set of rich family concepts, a kind of Wittgensteinian approach to family resemblances—and we must note the relation of Austin to Wittgenstein—that develops a force field around notions of the history of life-forms ("man", "women", "animal"), their political and juridical arrangements ("rights", "sovereignty", "crimes against humanity", "nation-state", "democracy") in relation to the emergence and development of the disciplines—notably "literature" and its cognate concepts—and the profession ("professor", "work" and so on). The "method" is familiar although not straightforwardly deconstructive; though certainly philosophical in the old "ordinary language" sense and strongly indebted, one might say governed, by the Austinian performative. The programmatic mapping simultaneously swings backwards and forwards; back to history and historical formations and forward to the new "humanities to come".

Before commenting further on Derrida's paper, I want to briefly invoke his past engagements with similar themes for they point to the *negative* imprint of "profession" and "performance": what Derrida's colleague Jean-François Lyotard (1984), drawing upon a combination of Austin and Luhmann, called "the logic of performativity" that, within the postmodern university, has resulted in a mere *professionalism* based upon a technical ideal of competence. The modern "liberal" university, caught in a pincer movement between the administrative apparatus of the state and the technical demands of the market, is now managed as an institution perpetually in crisis. Under the impact of global capitalism, with its huge investments in techno-science, the very concept of the modern university is also in crisis. Only the technological idea of excellence, it seems, can serve as the unifying idea (see Readings, 1996; Peters & Roberts, 1999).

Writing in response to this situation in the early 1980s and addressing Heidegger's notion of "the principle of reason" in relation to what he calls "the institution of modern techno-science," Derrida (1983: 11) asserted that the politics of research and teaching can no longer be reduced to a problematics centered on the nation-state but must take into account "networks that are apparently multi- or trans-national in form." For him, the Kantian distinction between the "technical" and the "architectonic" has been surpassed. In this transformed context, the concept of information integrates the basic to the applied and the purely rational to the technical. Against these tendencies, Derrida invoked a new responsibility to accompany the "rendering of reason." He suggests:

> It is not a matter simply of questions that one formulates while submitting oneself...to the principle of reason, but also of preparing oneself thereby to transform modes of writing, approaches to pedagogy, the procedures of academic exchange, the relations to other languages, to other disciplines, to the institution in general, to its inside and its outside. (Derrida, 1983: 17)

Derrida (1983: 17) argues that the new responsibility of "thought" cannot fail to be suspicious of a kind of professionalism of the university, which regulates university life according to the supply and demand of the market place and according to a purely technical ideal of competence. It is against these earlier statements and against Derrida's involvement in French educational policy and his establishment of the International Collège of Philosophy that we might begin to make sense of his positive rendering of the notion of profession and its future today.

Literalizing the University: Rorty on Derrida, Philosophy, and Literature

One of the consequences of Derrida's analysis is a set of criticisms that arises from what I call "the literalizing of the university," that is my shorthand for the centrality Derrida accords literature and the history of the concept of literature and its links with the performative "as if." For example, Rorty classifies of Derrida as a "private ironist" whose work as philosophy or literature has no public utility but rather fosters private forms of self-creation. Yet Derrida's self-description of his own project as an "enduring and constant interest towards that writing which is called literature" would seem to conflict with Rorty's reading. If, as Derrida argues, the history of literature cannot be separated from the history of democracy, then literature constitutes an *act of education* for it gains its political impetus from democratic rights, including freedom of speech. At the same time, literature in its modern sense develops in the late seventeenth century and becomes institutionalized only in the modern research university. Literature supersedes philosophy as the unifying discipline, responsible for *Bildung* and the development of cultural self-definition in terms of a national literature.

Rorty has written on Derrida with great authority and perspicacity. His account of deconstruction (Rorty, 1995a: 193) is one of the clearest of deconstruction both as a form of criticism and of its relation to radical politics. Rorty works on Heidegger as the key thinker to open up Derrida's philosophical tool-box. Deconstruction, like *Abbau* and *Destruktion* in Heidegger's philosophy, is part of a much more extensive philosophical vocabulary (such as *trace, différance, achi-écriture, supplement*) that signals a genuine post-metaphysical philosophy. What is more, he suggests that Derrida performs the service of teaching us how to free Heidegger's thought from the nostalgia, "sentimental pastoralism and nationalism" that led him to Nazism. By freeing him from his Nazi tendencies, Derrida thus, appropriates Heidegger for the Left. Rorty is persuasive when he suggests that post-human philosophers such as Heidegger and Derrida hint that new political possibilities will emerge when we accept that the language somehow "exceeds man." Deconstruction, thus, becomes a "perpetual self-destablizing activity" that constantly whittles away at "the metaphysical ideas presupposed by "humanistic ways of reading the traditional literary canon" (p. 194). As he writes:

> Those who practise deconstructive criticism typically see themselves as taking part in an activity which has much more to do with political change than with the "understanding" (much less the "appreciation") of what has traditionally been called "literature." (Rorty, 1995a: 193)

Rorty suggests that the term deconstruction, as a movement broader than literary criticism, functions as "a gesture in the direction of a groundswell of suspicion and impatience with the status quo among the intellectuals" (p. 196), in the same way that "socialism" functioned as a similar gesture towards an earlier groundswell for the preceding generation.

Rorty has written extensively on Derrida and in glowing terms (in addition to the essay referred to above, see Rorty, 1991, 1998a, 1998b). Yet Rorty, although an astute and careful interpreter of Derrida, has become increasingly uncomfortable with aspects of Derrida's work. As he argues in an engagement at a symposium designed to fathom how Derridean deconstruction and Rortyian pragmatism might contribute to articulating a non-foundationalist democracy:

> What pragmatists find most foreign in Derrida is his suspicion of empiricism, and naturalism—his assumption that these are forms of metaphysics, rather than replacements for metaphysics. (Rorty, 1996: 16)

And he continues:

> In my own writing about Derrida I have urged that we see him as sharing Dewey's utopian hopes, but not treat his work as contributing, in any clear or direct way, to these realization of these hopes. I divide philosophers, rather crudely, into those (like Mill, Dewey and Rawls) whose work fulfils primarily public purposes. I think of the Nietzsche-Heidegger-Derrida assault on metaphysics as producing private satisfactions to people who are deeply involved with philosophy (and therefore, necessarily, with metaphysics) but not as politically consequential, except in a very indirect and long-term way. (p. 16)

This was not the first time that Rorty had described Derrida in terms of the private. In *Contingency, Irony and Solidarity* (Rorty, 1989), he classifies Derrida as a "private ironist," denying that his work has anything to contribute to liberal political life. In a footnote to an essay "Habermas, Derrida, and the Functions of Philosophy" (Rorty, 1998c: fn 2, p. 307), a reworking of material excluded from *Contingency, Irony and Solidarity*, Rorty explains that the ironist, which contrasts with "metaphysician,"

> is a nominalist and historicist who strives to retain a sense that the vocabulary of moral deliberation she uses is a product of history and chance—of her having been born at a certain time in a certain place. The metaphysician, by contrast, believes that there is one right vocabulary of moral deliberation, one in touch with reality (and, in particular, with our essential humanity).

In *Contingency, Irony and Solidarity*, Rorty argued that:

> Heidegger's and Derrida's only relevance to the quest for social justice is that, like the Romantic poets before them, they make more vivid and concrete our sense of what human life might be like in a democratic utopia—a utopia in which the quest

for autonomy is impeded as little by social institutions. They do little to justify the choice of such a utopia or to hasten its arrival. But they do show how the creation of new discourses can enlarge the realm of possibility. They thereby help free us from the picture that gave rise to the philosophy of subjectivity in the first place—the metaphysician's picture of something deep within us, at the center of every human self, uncaused by and unreachable by historically conditioned processes of acculturation, something that privileges one vocabulary of moral deliberation over all others. (Rorty, 1989: 310–311)

For Rorty, the public and the private comprise two incommensurable vocabularies that cannot be reconciled. As Mouffe (1996: 3) puts it, "one where the desire for self-creation and autonomy dominates, and another one where what dominates is the desire for community." Rorty says that at the core of *Contingency, Irony and Solidarity*

is a distinction between private concerns, in the sense of idiosyncratic projects of self-overcoming, and public concerns, those having to do with the suffering of other being beings. This distinction is emphatically not the one with which some readers (notably feminist critics, such as Nancy Fraser) have identified it: the distinction between the domestic heath and the public forum, between *oikos* and *polis*. (Rorty, 1989: fn2, 307–308)

For Rorty, there are no guarantees for liberal politics; there is no viewpoint that can demonstrate the superiority of democracy; and, the project of Kantian-inspired philosophers such as Habermas who seemingly want to derive a universalistic moral philosophy justifying liberal democracy from the nature of language is just simply wrong-headed. We should, according to Rorty, "peel apart Enlightenment liberalism from Enlightenment rationalism" (Rorty, 1995b: 22) for democracy depends not on a theory of truth but rather on a set of pragmatic moves designed to change our democratic practices by persuading people to build a more inclusive community. As Mouffe (1996: 5) puts it:

For Rorty, it is through sentiment and sympathy, not through rationality and universalistic moral discourse, that democratic advances take place. This is why he considers books like *Uncle Tom's Cabin* to have played a more important role than philosophical treatises in securing moral progress.

On Rorty's understanding, Derrida's works, both his earlier "philosophical" works and his more recent literary ones, have little to do with democracy or education. They have little if any public utility at all for they should be seen primarily as concerning private projects of self-creation and overcoming.

Derrida has recently responded to Rorty's criticisms. In *Contingency, Irony and Solidarity*, Rorty (1989) proposes the distinction between "private ironist" and "public liberal," consigning Derrida to the former category and arguing that his work has no political consequences, a claim he repeats in *Deconstruction and Pragmatism*:

> I divide philosophers, rather crudely, into those (like Mill, Dewey and Rawls) whose work fulfils primarily public purposes, and those whose work fulfils primarily private purposes. I think of the Nietzsche-Heidegger-Derrida assault on metaphysics as producing private satisfactions to people who are deeply involved with philosophy (and therefore, necessarily, with metaphysics) but not as politically consequential, *except in a very indirect and long-term way* (Rorty, 1996: 16, my emphasis).

While Rorty (1998a: 138) acknowledges that he considers Derrida to be a "romantic utopian"—a label that Derrida rejects in favor of the "messianic"— he also suggests that "a revival of ineffability" is linked to a "principled, theorized, philosophical hopelessness" of the Left (p. 37). His answer is to relegate Derrida to private life insofar as he offers "a quasi-religious form of spiritual pathos" (p. 96).

Derrida, himself, in response to Rorty—while accepting much else of Rorty's description of his work—rejects Rorty's public/private distinction as applying to his work by suggesting that his more literary texts "are not evidence of a retreat towards the private, they are performative problematizations of the public/private distinction" (Derrida, 1996: 79). Literature in the way Derrida studies or practices it, he suggests, is "the complete opposite of the expression of private life." "Literature," he continues, "is a public institution of recent invention," defined in terms of its European history by "the principled authorization that anything can be said publicly" (Derrida, 1996: 80).

Derrida, the University, and the Ends of Literature

Perhaps, the clearest and most direct statement of Derrida's on his own project comes from a text that he presented in 1980 at the opening of his thesis defense based on published works.[1] In this work entitled "The Time of a Thesis: Punctuations" (Derrida, 1983), he indicates that around 1957, in a context marked by Husserl's thought, he registered his first thesis topic as "The Ideality of the Literary Object" and he says that his "most constant interest, coming even before my philosophical interest I should say, if this is possible, had been directed towards literature, towards that writing which is called literary" (p. 37). Derrida directs himself not only to the question "what is literature?" but also to "what is it "to write?"" that is,

> When and how does an inscription become literature and what takes place when it does? To what and to whom is this due? What takes place between philosophy and literature, science and literature, politics and literature, theology and literature, psychoanalysis and literature. (pp. 37–38)

As J. Hillis Miller (2001: 62–63) remarks, literature for Derrida has "no pure originality" or hidden essence. Any piece of language can be read as literature but to do so "involves that complex set of conventions, rules, institutions, and historical features that are both within the text and within the mind of the one who performs the act (a speech act) of taking a given text as literature." He continues:

> More broadly speaking, just what, for Derrida, are the rules, conventions, and institutions that define the "literary character of the text"? Derrida gives a specific and somewhat surprising answer to that question. Literature as an institution in the West, says Derrida, is linked to democracy and to freedom of speech, the freedom, in principle, though never of course in fact, to say or write anything, or to perform any symbolic act. This means that literature, as an institution in the West, has a quite short history. It arose with Western-style democracies, in the late seventeenth century, and would disappear if they disappeared. (p. 63)

This passage explains, in part, why Derrida takes issue with Rorty's description of his work and focuses precisely on the private/public distinction and the way he applies it to his work as literature. He wants to dispute Rorty's assessment not only on the distinction between philosophy and literature but also on the role literature plays in relation to the private/public distinction:

> Literature interests me, supposing that, in my own way, I practise it or that I study it in others, precisely as something which is the complete opposite of the expression of private life. Literature is a public institution of recent invention, with a comparatively short history, governed by all sorts of conventions connected to the evolution of law, which allows, in principle, anything to be said. Thus, what defines literature as such, within a certain European history, is profoundly connected with a revolution in law and politics: the principled authorization that anything can be said publicly. In other words, I am not able to separate the invention of literature, the history of literature, from the history of democracy. (pp. 79–80)

If the invention of literature cannot be separated from the history of democracy—and if the connection between the development of a literary culture, a reading public, and civil society or the so-called public sphere cannot be broken—then, the connection must be made also between literature, democracy, and higher education. Literacy, national literatures as vehicles for cultural self-definition of the nation-state, and civil liberties, including freedom of speech, were associated with the gradual development and extension of a universal education. Indeed, the concept of literature in the modern sense becomes established only with the appearance of the research university in the early nineteenth century, when the study of literature becomes institutionalized and the mantle of the responsibility for *Bildung* is handed over from philosophy to literature (Readings, 1996).

At the same time, under the pressure of globalization and the technological transformation of communication, we might say "the end of literature is at hand." As Hillis Miller (2002: 1) explains:

> The end of literature is at hand. Literature's time is almost up. It is about time. It is about, that is, the different epochs of different media. Literature, in spite of its approaching end, is nevertheless perennial and universal. It will survive all historical and technological changes. Literature is a feature of any human culture at any time and place. These two contradictory premises must govern all serious reflection "on literature" these days.

Yet the process of ending is also a point of historical transformation. As Miller (2000: n.p.) points out by reference to Derrida, "the new regime of telecommunications is bringing literature to an end by transforming all those factors that were its preconditions or its concomitants." As he explains further, "The concept of literature in the West has been inextricably tied to Cartesian notions of selfhood, to the regime of print, to Western-style democracies and notions of the nation-state, and to the right to free speech within such democracies" (n.p.). It is precisely these conditions and the old inside/outside dichotomies on which they are based that are problematized by the new regime of telecommunications. It is this sense of the public, and by implication, the private, that Derrida's *The Post Card* gently ironizes: the postcard is both "an old-fashioned remnant of the rapidly disappearing culture of handwriting, print, and the postal system" as well as "a proleptic anticipation of the publicity and openness of the new communications regimes" (Miller, 2000: n.p.). In a paragraph that deserves full citation, Miller provides the following commentary, germane to our purposes:

> Derrida expresses his sense of the way the new regime of telecommunications brings about the decline of the nation state (about which we hear so much these days) as well

as a transformation of the individual's sense of identity and privacy. Derrida stresses the strange combination of solitude and a new kind of being with others of the person using a computer to reach the World Wide Web, as well as the breakdown of traditional boundaries between inside and outside brought about by new communication technologies. As this epochal cultural displacement from the book age to the hypertext age has accelerated we have, in Derrida's view, been ushered ever more rapidly into a threatening living space. This new electronic space, the space of television, cinema, telephone, videos, fax, e-mail, hypertext, and the Internet, has profoundly altered the economies of the self, the home, the workplace, the university, and the nation-state's politics. These were traditionally ordered around the firm boundaries of an inside-outside dichotomy, whether those boundaries were the walls between the home's privacy and all the world outside or the borders between the nation-state and its neighbours. The new technologies invade the home and the nation. They confound all these inside/outside divisions.

Thus, the new teletechnologies not only bring the Other into our private spaces, they also undermine traditional ideas of the self as unified. They work to dislocate not only traditional ideas of the unified self, but also other unities, and especially the unities of our institutions—the national literature, the university, democracy. They also disassemble the idea that the self is unified precisely because it occupies a secure spatiotemporal location in the grid or system of reference, anchored by a particular culture-bound place, often nationalist sentiments of "one-culture, one-language, one-nation," sometimes a more encompassing and less politically threatening single "national culture" with its territory, its boundaries, and "its ethnic and cultural unity."

Derrida calls this set of assumptions the *ontopolitopologique*. Miller acknowledges this assumption and then quotes and translates Derrida as follows:

> a new and powerful advance in the technological pros-thesis that, in a thousand ways, ex-propriates, de-localizes, de-territorializes, extirpates, that is to say, in the etymological and therefore radical sense of this word, uproots, therefore de-etymologizes, dissociates the political from the topological, separates from itself what has always been the very concept of the political, that is, what links the political to the topical, to the city, to the territory, to the ethno-national frontier. (Derrida cited in Miller, 2000, n.p.)

These are themes that Derrida has now consistently developed elsewhere (e.g., Derrida, 1994a; Derrida & Stiegler, 2002). For instance, in an interview with Richard Beardsworth, he talks in Nietzschean terms of *democracy to come*. As Beardsworth observes, the promise of democracy is not the same as either the *fact* of democracy or the regulative *idea* (in the Kantian sense) of democracy. On Derrida's account of *difference*, we might expect deconstruction to challenge, perhaps, heavily centralist and "structured" representationalist models of democracy and to favor a greater recognition of difference and the Other—possibly even, in conjunction with these emphases, an emphasis on the promotion of local autonomy and greater global world democracy.

Postscript: The Postcolonial University

I take it that the legacy of Nietzsche's critique of modernity for Derrida is to point us towards recognizing the twin dangers to the university and to understanding German idealism and the Kantian idea of the university in a critical sense within a context transformed by global capitalism. This theme is creatively explored in terms of the performative acts of profession and the humanities as the site and production of performative "works" in the sense of *oeuvres* rather than *travail*. Nietzsche's critique also, I think, impels us to analyze the different nationalist forms and historical models of the university in their own native traditions, not least in order to understand their colonial and postcolonial manifestations (see Peters, 1997). Perhaps, more affirmatively, Nietzsche's legacy offers some signposts for the future by steering us back, against the anti-traditionalism of modernity to ruminate over and question our historical sources of cultural renewal—not only Oxford, Paris, and Bologna, but also Athens and Alexandria—so that we might in future define different institutions upon a reevaluation of old values, or new institutions out of different values.

This is what Jacques Derrida analyses when he writes of "the teleological axis" of the Kantian discourse that builds upon the Greek *polis* to talk of *cosmopolis* in a way that has become characteristic of European modernity. While,

> A philosopher is always someone for whom philosophy is not given, someone who in essence must question him or herself about the essence and destination of philosophy. (Derrida, 1994a: 3)

It is also the case that:

> Philosophy has never been the unfolding responsible for a unique, originary assignation linked to a unique language or to the place of a sole people. *Philosophy does not have one sole memory.* Under its Greek name and in its European memory it has always been bastard, hybrid, grafted, multilinear and polyglot. (p. 6)

As of philosophy and the philosopher, so too of the idea and the institution of university and the profession. In this look back, it is important to take stock of the contemporary discourse of *Internationalization*. Internationalization is a set of processes in search of a theory and/or concept of internationalism yet to be articulated. Internationalization most often figures as a discourse of strategy with an emphasis on "how to" questions rather than a reflective discourse examining political ends or purposes. Yet internationalization as a set of processes has changed over time, most recently reflecting changes in the political economy of higher education and in the global economy. There are different forms of internationalization that differ according to the colonial past, geopolitics, and global position—so we should talk of "internationalizations" (in the plural). In this respect, we might talk of internationalization *before* globalization. Internationalization took place in the ancient world with the first academies in Pakistan, India, Egypt, China and Persia (Takshashila, Nalanda, Al-Azhar, Yuelu, Gandishapur) in the seventh and ninth centuries BC that attracted students from all over Asia and Middle East. The Academy was established by Plato in 387 BC (but we should remember also Kos, Rhodes, and Alexandria) and traveling "itinerant" scholars—Sophists (Protagoras, Gorgias, Prodicus, Hippias) wandered about Greece teaching rhetoric. First wave of internationalization took place in Europe during the period of the establishment of the medieval university (Magnaura, 849; Salerno, ninth century; Bologna, 1088; Paris, 1100) and the cathedral schools established by papal bull.

Translation can be considered as a form of internationalization with a spread of texts into Arabic during the "Golden Age" (750–950) of Muslim scholarship and into Latin with the great revival of Greek texts fueled by the proliferation of texts from the East in fifteenth-century Italy that exerted an influence on sixteenth-century Britain. A history of internationalization in the ancient world needs to take into account a complex set of movements that emphasize the interrelationships between trade, conquest, and traveling scholarship, including, for example, at the following moments: the Hellenization of Syria and the founding of Gandishapur as a center of learning (how Greek science passed to the Arabic world); Christianity as a Hellenizing force and Christian Syriac writers, scholars, and scientists; the Nestorians and the Monophysites; the Indian influence, Alexandrian science, the sea route to northwest India, and Buddhism as a possible medium spreading west; Khalifates of Damascus and Baghdad (762) and early Arabic translators (*Abu Mahammad Ibn al-Muqaffa', Al-Hajjaj Ibn Yusuf Ibn Matar Al-Hasib, Yuhanna Ibn Batriq, 'Abd al-Masih Ibn 'Aballah Wa'ima al-Himse, Abu Yahya al-Batriq, Jibra'il II, Abu Zakariah Yahya Ibn Masawaih*) who translated Buddhist and Greek texts, including Euclid's *Elements*, Aristotle's *Poetica*, Ptolemy's *Tetrabiblos*, Galen's texts, and so on.

At the same time, we must take account of the complex processes of colonization based on the export of the form of the university, resistance to the colonial form, and later not only indigenization of the university but also the indigenous university.[2] How might the development and humanization of the new humanities—which grows out of a Eurocentric culture and now is modulated according to the new keys of digitalization and virtualization (even as Derrida says "mondialization")—make room for the humanity of other cultures? How might such unconditionality of the university restyle the concept of man, add to the history of truth, and contribute to producing new events to transform the colonial and postcolonial university into a place of resistance?

Notes

1. For other autobiographical "takes" on his intellectual life, see Bennington & Derrida, 1999; Derrida, 1995; and Derrida & Ferraris, 2001.
2. I am thinking of the "Zapatista" University near San Cristobel in Chiapas I visited briefly in 2006 and also the Maori universities in Aotearoa/New Zealand. See, for instance, *Te Whare Wananga o Awanuiarangi* that carries a *Mihi* on its website with the following "We commit ourselves to explore and define the depths of bicultural knowledge in Aotearoa—to enable us to rediscover ourselves, to know who we are, to know where we come from and to claim our own place in the millennium ahead. We take this journey of discovery, of reclamation of sovereignty; establishing the equality of Maori intellectual tradition alongside the knowledge base of others. Thus, we can stand proudly together with all people of the world" http://www.wananga.ac.nz/.

References

Bennington, G. & Derrida, J. (1999) *Jacques Derrida*, Geoffrey Bennington (trans.). Chicago & London: University of Chicago Press.

Derrida, J. (1983) "The Principle of Reason: University in the Eyes of Its Pupils," *Diacritics*, Fall, 3–20.

Derrida, J. (1994a) "Nietzsche and the Machine: An Interview with Jacques Derrida by Richard Beardsworth," *Journal of Nietzsche Studies*, 7: 7–66.

Derrida, J. (1994b) "Of the Humanities and the Philosophical Discipline: The Right to Philosophy from the Cosmopolitical Point of View," *Surfaces*, 4.

Derrida, J. (1994c) *Specters of Marx: The State of the Debt, the Work of Mourning, & the New International*. Peggy Kamuf (trans.). London: Routledge.

Derrida, J. (1996) "Remarks on Deconstruction and Pragmatism," in Chantal Mouffe (ed.), *Deconstruction and Pragmatism*. London & New York: Routledge. pp. 77–88.

Derrida, J. (1997) *Politics of Friendship*, George Collins (trans.). London: Verso Books.

Derrida, J. (2001) "The future of the profession or the university without condition (thanks to the 'Humanities', what could take place tomorrow)," Peggy Kamuf (trans.) In: L. Simmons and H.Worth (eds.), *Derrida Downunder*. Palmerston North (NZ): Dunmore Press: 233–48. A version also appears in Deconstructing Derrida: Tasks for the New Humanities. Peter Pericles Trifonas and Michael A. Peters (eds.), New York: Palgrave MacMillan, pp. 11–24.

Derrida, J. & Stiegler, B. (2002) *Echographies of Television: Filmed Interviews*, Jennifer Bajorek (trans.). Cambridge: Polity Press.

Le Goff, J. (1991) *Pour un autre Moyen Age*. Paris: Gallimard.

Lyotard J.-F. (1984) *The Postmodern Condition: A Report On Knowledge*. G. Bennington & B. Massumi (trans.), Foreword by Fredric Jameson. Minneapolis: University of Minnesota Press; Manchester: University of Manchester Press.

Miller, J.H. (2000) "'Stay! Speak, Speak. I Charge Thee, Speak,' An Interview by Wang Fengzhen and Shaobo Xie," *Culture Machine*, available at: (http://culturemachine.tees.ac.uk/Cmach/Backissues/j002/Articles/art_mIller.htm)

Miller, J.H. (2001) "Derrida and Literature," in Tom Cohen (ed.), *Jacques Derrida and the Humanities: A Critical Reader*. Cambridge: Cambridge University Press.

Miller, J.H. (2002) *On Literature*. London: Routledge.

Mouffe, C. (1996) "Deconstruction, Pragmatism and the Politics of Democracy," in Chantal Mouffe (ed.), *Deconstruction and Pragmatism*. London and New York: Routledge, pp. 13–18.

Nietzsche, F. (1968[1888]) *Twilight of the Idols; and, The Anti-Christ* (trans. with an introduction and commentary, by R.J. Hollingdale). Harmondsworth: Penguin.

Peters, M.A. (ed.) (1997) *Cultural Politics and the University*. Palmerston North (NZ): Dunmore Press.

Peters, M.A. (2000) "Nietzsche and the Critique of Modernity," in Peters, M.A. Marshall, J.D., & Smeyers, P. (eds.), *Past and Present Values: Nietzsche's Legacy for Education*. Westport, CT. & London: Bergin and Garvey.

Peters, M.A. & Roberts, P. (1999) *University Futures and the Politics of Reform in New Zealand*. Palmerston North (NZ): Dunmore Press.

Readings, B. (1996) *The University in Ruins*. Cambridge, MA/London: Harvard University Press.

Rifkin, J. (1995) *The End of Work—The Decline of the Global Labor Force and the Dawn of the Post-Market Era*. New York: Tarcher/Putnam.

Rorty, R. (1989) *Contingency, Irony, and Solidarity*. Cambridge & New York: Cambridge University Press.

Rorty, R. (1991) "Is Derrida a Transcendental Philosopher?" In *Essays on Heidegger and Others: Philosophical Papers*, Vol. 2. Cambridge: Cambridge University Press. pp. 119–128.

Rorty, R. (1995) "Deconstruction," in Raman Selden (ed.), *The Cambridge History of Literary Criticism: From Formalism to Poststructuralism*. Cambridge, UK: Cambridge University Press.

Rorty, R. (1996) "Remarks on Deconstruction and Pragmatism," in Mouffe, Chantal (ed.), *Deconstruction and Pragmatism*. London & New York: Routledge. pp. 13–18.

Rorty, R. (1998a) *Achieving our Country: Leftist Thought in Twentieth-Century America*. Cambridge, MA: Harvard University Press.

Rorty, R. (1998b) "Derrida and the Philosophical Tradition," in *Truth and Progress: Philosophical Papers*. Cambridge: Cambridge University Press. pp. 327–356.

Rorty, R. (1998c) "Habermas, Derrida, and the Functions of Philosophy," in *Truth and Progress: Philosophical Papers*. Cambridge: Cambridge University Press. pp. 307–326.

WELCOME! POSTSCRIPT ON HOSPITALITY, COSMOPOLITANISM, AND THE OTHER

MICHAEL A. PETERS

> Hospitality is culture itself and not simply one ethic amongst others. Insofar as it has to do with the ethos, that is, the residence, one's at-home, the familiar place of dwelling, as much as the manner of being there, the manner in which we relate to ourselves and to others, to others as our own or as foreigners, ethics is hospitality; ethics is entirely coextensive with the experience of hospitality, whichever way one expands or limits that.
> —Jacques Derrida, On Cosmopolitanism and Forgiveness, 2001, pp. 16–17.

One of the most promising approaches to understanding the ethical issues at stake in current notions and practices of cultural exchange that inform globalization, cosmopolitanism, immigration, internationalization, and study abroad is that provided by Derrida's Paris seminar on the theme of hospitality at the Ecole des Hautes Etudes en Sciences Sociales given in 1996 where he develops a set of related concepts tying hospitality to "friendship," "forgiveness," and "the gift."[1] His seminar, now a kind of pedagogical institution in itself, also maps the development of his thought in a series of related texts. At the same time, the seminar on hospitality provides a context for raising a range of related questions concerning national and ethnic identity, citizenship, and immigration, all in close proximity to the ethics and politics of the Other.

Derrida's network of concepts produces a novel ethical space in which to revisit the Kantian liberal notion of cosmopolitanism within the context of globalization and to raise fresh questions about "our" openness to the Other—also about segregation, separation, and exclusion as social and policy instruments of "othering."[2] Derrida's late philosophy of hospitality, although not easy to read or understand, promises an approach suited to understanding the discourse of the Other and many of the underlying ethical issues that trouble existing practices and justifications of cosmopolitanism, globalization, internationalization, world citizenship, and immigration. It serves as a pedagogy of the Other that is also a deep or profound humanism.

Derrida's understanding of "hospitality" is colored by the uniqueness of his own personal experience as a French Jew born into a family that had lived in Algeria for many years. David Carroll, a colleague at the University of California at Irvine, describes in memoriam Derrida's uncomfortable identity caught between Arab Algerian and French colonialist communities and excluded by Vichy government by the fact of his Jewishness:

> Jacques Derrida was born in El-Biar, Algeria on July 15, 1930 into a family that had lived in Algeria for centuries before its conquest and colonization by the French. His grandparents had become French citizens in 1870, when the *Crémieux Decree* granted citizenship to the Jewish population of Algeria, who, like its Arab and Berber inhabitants, had until then been considered French subjects with limited civil and legal rights. Jacques described more than once the effect on him of arriving at school one day at the age of 12 to be told that he could no longer attend classes. He had been excluded from the French public school system because of the severe *Numerus Clausus* imposed on Jewish students after the Vichy collaborationist government rescinded citizenship for all Algerian Jews. He was able to return to school a year after the arrival of Allied troops in North Africa, but never forgot how it felt to be a victim of discrimination, deprived of basic civil rights, and treated as an unwanted foreigner in his own land; to realize, as he put it, that he was a citizen of no country at all. (http://www.universityofcalifornia.edu/senate/inmemoriam/JacquesDerrida.htm)

In a recent paper, Carroll (2006)—inspired by Derrida's remarks on his "remains" of Algeria, what remains in his identity and work—considers Derrida's experience as an "other" connecting it to his view of the arbitrariness and accidental nature of citizenship and its relation to systematic exclusions of certain peoples. He begins by referring to Derrida's (1998) own reflections on his loss of citizenship in *Monolingualism of the Other* that is important to cite in this context:

> A supposedly "ethnic" or "religious" group that finds itself one day deprived, as a group, of citizenship by a state that, with the brutality of a unilateral decision, withdraws it without asking for their opinion, and *without the said group gaining back any*

other citizenship. No other. Now I have experienced that. Along with others, I lost then recovered my French citizenship. I lost it for years without having any other. None at all, you see.... And then, one day, "one fine day," without once again having requested anything, and still too young to know it with a properly political knowledge, I found my aforementioned citizenship again. The state, to which I had never spoken, had returned it to me.... The withdrawal of French citizenship from the Jews of Algeria, with everything that followed, was the work of the French alone. They decided it all by themselves, in their heads; they must have been dreaming about it all along; they implemented it all by themselves. I was very young at that time, and I certainly did not understand very well...what citizenship and the loss of citizenship *mean*. (1998: 15–16, trans. modified [34–35])

Carroll (2006: 908) comments:

What is "learned" from the loss of citizenship, without ever understanding exactly what is meant by the term, is the precarious, arbitrary, artificial nature of citizenship and national identity, that they are not in any sense "natural." What is experienced are the destructive effects of exclusion, of being put in the place of the other, the outsider who is declared by law not to be in his proper place even in the place where he has always been, the indigenous alien who is not granted the same basic rights as others who inhabit the same place. It is to learn what it is to be "hostage" to others in one's own home, in this case, hostage to the French in one's native land [*pays*]. This is something, Derrida admits, that always remained with him.

Influenced by Levinas and the priority he accords to ethics and to an absolute form of hospitality that exists prior to politics, Derrida forges an ethics as responsibility to the Other based on a series of possible and impossible aporias—hospitality, the gift, forgiveness, mourning—that in themselves transcend and avoid the common assumption in liberal accounts "that responsibility is to be associated with behavior that accords with general principles capable of justification in the public realm" (Reynolds, 2006, http://www.iep.utm.edu/d/derrida.htm#H6). Reynolds' discussion of Derrida's approach to the Other is both insightful and instructive not only in terms of elaborating "responsibility to the other" and the injunction of Abrahamic principal of "radical singularity" before God, but also in terms of the account of the "wholly Other/Messianic" that taps the Judaic tradition and points that "the *messianic* structure of existence is open to the coming of an entirely ungraspable and unknown other" as well as that "the concrete, historical *messianisms* are open to the coming of a specific other of known characteristics" (ibid.).

"Hospitality," for Derrida, thus, has a rich religiophilosophical significance and complexity that motivates his pedagogy in the seminars and in his writings of the last decade. Gil Anidjar (2001), in "A Note on Hostipitality," suggests:

> The thread of hospitality—here explicitly linked to forgiveness and friendship, to humor and transcendence—can be followed in Derrida's work since at least *Writing and Difference*, most notably, though not exclusively, in his readings of Levinas. It has emerged in a more explicit fashion in *Politics of Friendship*, *Adieu to Emmanuel Levinas*, and recently in *Of Hospitality* (which includes two earlier sessions of Derrida's seminar on hospitality). But who or what is the subject of hospitality? To one reading of this question, the French language provides a disarmingly and qualitatively simple answer: the *hôte*. In French, the hote is both the one who gives, *donne*, and the one who received *reçoit*, hospitality. As Derrida argues, however, this distinction finds its condition in the aporetic laws of hospitality that prior to either, give both hotes the possibility and the impossibility of the gift of hospitality. (p. 356)

He concludes that Derrida's neologism *hostipitalité* "raises in a radically new way the question of the subject of hospitality." It is to be located in an aporia, a puzzle or paradox that harnesses an impossibility reconciliation between two contradictory imperatives: (1) the imperative to welcome the Other in an absolute or unconditional sense before the knowledge or recognition that comes with names or understanding identity and (2) the imperative to welcome someone in particular, someone who might pose a threat to us or even to whom we might refuse entry to our home. As Derrida (2003) himself expresses unconditional hospitality,

> But pure or unconditioned hospitality does not consist in such an invitation ("I invite you, I welcome you into my home, on the condition that you adapt to the laws and norms of my territory, according to my language, tradition, memory, and so on"). Pure and unconditional hospitality, hospitality itself, opens or is in advance open to someone who is neither expected nor invited, to whomever arrives as an absolutely foreign visitor, as a new arrival, nonidentifiable and unforeseeable, in short, wholly other. (p. 17)

In "Hostipitality," Derrida (2000) investigates a reading of Kant's cosmopolitanism given in the third article of *Perpetual Peace* that stipulates "Cosmopolitan Right shall be limited to Conditions of Universal Hospitality." As Derrida explains:

> In this context hospitality [Hospitalität (Wirtbarkeit)] means the right of a stranger [bedeutet das Recht eines Fremdlings] not to be treated with hostility [en ennemi] when he arrives on someone else's territory [seiner Ankunft auf der Boden eines andern wegen von diesem nicht feindselig behandelt zu werden] (p. 2).

And he goes on to argue:

> Two words are underlined by Kant in this title: "cosmopolitan right" [Weltbürgerrecht: the right of world citizens]—we are thus in the space of right, not of morality and politics or anything else but of a right determined in its relation to citizenship, the state, the subject of the state, even if it is a world state—it is a question therefore of an international right; the other underlined word is "hospitality" [der allgemeinen Hospitalität, universal hospitality]. It is a question therefore of defining the conditions of a cosmopolitan right, of a right the terms of which would be established by a treaty between states, by a kind of UN charter before the fact, and one of these conditions would be what Kant calls universal hospitality, die allgemeine Hospitalität. (p. 3)

Yet this liberal cosmopolitan right will not suffice. In order to truly resolve all conflict and otherness, I have to welcome the Other unconditionally, that is, without prior knowledge of the Other or without a name, indeed, without documents such as a passport. This unconditionality implies a total *openness*—of house, of being, of culture—to the Other, an ethical relation that is transgressive in its overcoming of conditions either religious as in the Judeo-Christian understanding of hospitality, or political as in Kant's reference to citizenship and the state. Derrida stands in direct opposition to the anthropological and ethnological tradition. It is a tradition that Derrida take issue with: exchange in "primitive societies" (as Mauss, Boas and Malinowski termed them) was understood in anthropological terms under the description of "the gift" but this description does not accurately analyze the cultural practice nor its place, role and status. Rather it tends to reflect more about the moralizing intention of the author—imbued by the French Romantic tradition of the "noble savage" and anxious to counterpose a "primitive" and ancestral generosity against the contemporary capitalist "selfish" hoarding exchange. Liberal socialist ideological beliefs thus structure the depiction of past cultural practices of exchange in ways that enable anthropologist to castigate the present emphasis on forms of individualist egoism.

Derrida's profound humanism is a deconstruction of those early anthropological accounts to substitute an ethic of hospitality that is the very ground of ethics and of relation to the Other which at the same time constitutes the basis and condition for pedagogy, and especially for pedagogy within a dynamic multicultural globalism.

Notes

1. This Postscript is based on a section of an unpublished paper "Cultural Exchange, Study Abroad and the Discourse of the Other" by Michael A. Peters and Shivali Tukdeo.
2. I use the term "our" openness here to mean the West and in particular the European (and American) encounters as colonizers of the "new world" with first nations peoples and with the colonized. I realize this is a very broad approach but it does have the advantage of at least registering the ethnocentrism of my "our."

References

Carroll, D. (2006) "Remains" of Algeria: Justice, Hospitality, Politics. *MLN*, 121(4) September 2006 (French Issue): 808–827.

Derrida, J. (1997a) *Adieu a Emmanuel Levinas*. Paris: Galilee.

Derrida, J. (1997b) *The Politics of Friendship*, G. Collins (trans.). London: Verso.

Derrida, J. (1998) *Monolingualism of the Other: Or the Prothesis of Origin*, P. Menash (trans.). Stanford, CA: Stanford University Press.

Derrida, J. (2000) Hostipitality. B. Stocker & F. Morlock (trans.), *Angelaki, Journal of the Theoretical Humanities*, 5(3) (December): 3–18.

Derrida, J. (2001) *On Cosmopolitanism and Forgiveness*. London: Routledge.

Derrida, J. (2003) Autoimmunity: Real and Symbolic Suicides. A Dialogue with Jacques Derrida, pp. 85–136 ; Deconstructing Terrorism, pp. 137–172. In: *Philosophy in a Time of Terror*. Giovanna Borradori (ed.). Chicago: Chicago University Press.

Derrida, J. (2005) The Principle of Hospitality: An Interview with Dominique Dhombres. *Le Monde*, December 2, 1997. Ashley Thompson (trans.), *Parallax*, 11(1): 6–9.

Derrida, J., & Dufourmantelle, A. (2000) *Of Hospitality*, R. Bowlby (trans.). Stanford, CA: Stanford University Press (Original work published in 1997).

Derrida, J. & Roudinesco, E. (2004) *For What Tomorrow...*, J. Fort (trans.). Stanford, CA: Stanford University Press (Original work published in 2001).

Gil A. (2001) "A Note on Hostipitality," in J. Derrida (ed.), *Acts of Religion*. New York: London.

INDEX

academia
    Derrida blamed for crisis in, 65
    See also humanities; university
Achieving Our Country (Rorty), 7
Albert, Hans, 84, 87
Algeria, 134
alterity, Western philosophy's inability to recognize, 28
Althusser, Louis, 69, 70
American Memory (Cheney), 51
Anidjar, Gil, 136
Anthropologie Structurale (Lévi-Strauss), 61
The Anti-Christ (Nietzsche), 50
antihumanism, 63-64, 65
anti-Nietzscheans, 65
Apel, Karl-Otto, 85-88, 92
"apology," 45-46
aporia of urgency, 34
Archive Fever (Derrida), 54
argumentation, 86, 87, 92
Aristotle, 82
assessment, 107
Austin, J.L., 105, 106, 119
autonomy, rational, 99-100
Un autre Moyen Age (Le Goff), 117

Bataille, Georges, 41
Bayle, Pierre, 82

Beardsworth, Richard, 73, 127
Being and Time (Heidegger), 71
belief, distinction with knowledge, 81-82
Bernstein, Richard, 15
Beuys, Joseph, 110-11
Beyond Good and Evil (Nietzsche), 50, 115
Blanchot, Maurice, 71
bloggers, reaction to Derrida's death by, 3-4
Bloom, Alan, 50-51

California, University of at Irvine, 2, 47
Cambridge University, 4-5, 43, 65
Caputo, J.D., 16, 32, 91
Carroll, David, 134, 135
Cheney, Lynne, 51
Christian Cause, 48
citizenship, 134-35
classroom, grammatological, 110
colonialism
    Derrida's experience with, 53, 134
    Enlightenment's alliance with, 52-53
    and export of form of university, 130
    and humanism, 53
    Said's experience with, 53
communication
    and end of literature, 126
    as event, 106

maintained by act of exclusion, 18
misunderstanding in, 18, 105-7
technological transformation of, 126
community of communication, 86
community of communication, ideal, 86, 88, 92
"A Concept of Critical Thinking" (Ennis), 82-83
confession, 117, 118
constative acts, 119
content in education, 66-67
Contingency, Irony, and Solidarity (Rorty), 122-24
cosmopolitanism, 133-34, 136-37
crimes against humanity, 118
criterion
    in critical dogmatism, 84
    in transcendental critique, 83
critical dogmatism, 83, 84-85, 87, 88, 91-92
Critical Theory Archive, 47
critical thinking, 82-83
critique, 81-82, 83, 84
    See also critical dogmatism; critical thinking; critique, transcendental
critique, transcendental, 83, 85-88
Cullenberg, Stephen, 41
curriculum, core, 66-67

Dasein, 61, 70-71
death
Derrida on, 2-3
Derrida's, 1, 3-4
decisions, ethical, 34-35
"The Decline and Fall of French Nietzscheo-Structuralism" (Engel), 65-66
Deconstructing Derrida (Trifonas and Peters), 40
deconstruction
    as act of defiance toward Eurocentrism, 54
    as affirmation of other, 15-16, 29, 90, 91
    as affirmative, 15-16
    allegations against, 15, 64-69
    American reception of, 60
    Bloom on, 50-51
    critical work of, 93
    difference with critical dogmatism, 91-92
    difference with transcendental critique, 92-93
    and education, 33-34
    ethicopolitical horizon of, 15
    explanation of, 8-9, 44, 121
    Gutmann's criticisms of, 66-68
    interpreted as skeptical position, 17
    as inventionalism, 16
    and justice, 30, 34, 103
    and metaphysics, 30, 44
    "method" of, 89-90
    object of critique, 89
    occurrence of, 30
    as reaction to Münchhausen Trilemma, 89
    reconstruction of subject by, 69
    reflexivity of, 30
    relation of understanding and misunderstanding in, 18-19
    relevance to education, 9
    relevance to pedagogy, 9
    as a response, 28
    Rorty's account of, 121
Deconstruction and Pragmatism (Rorty), 124
Deconstruction and the Possibility of Justice (Derrida), 31
Delacampagne, Christian, 46
democracy
    Derrida accused of threatening workable notion of, 59-60, 62
    Derrida on, 73-74
    Derrida on Nietzsche's views of, 72-73
    Ferry and Renaut on, 68-69
    history of, 118
    and literature, 125-26
    and media, 73, 74
    need to think of in global terms, 74
    Nietzsche in relation to, 68-69
    Rorty on, 123
    and technology, 73-74
democracy to come, 73, 74, 127
Derrida, Jacques

alleged lack of public consequences of, 122-24
Archive Fever, 54
attacks against, 65-66
attempts of to renew humanistic scholarship, 52, 53-55
citations of, 42-43
contributions to post-Nietzschean philosophy of university, 116
On Cosmopolitanism and Forgiveness, 39
death of, 1, 3-4
Deconstruction and the Possibility of Justice, 31
definition of justice, 103
description of own project, 121, 124-25
Dissemination, 23
"The Ends of Man," 44, 61, 63
establishment of International Collège of Philosophy, 120
exclusion, experience with, 134-35
Ferry and Renaut's criticisms of, 64
"Forgiving the Unforgivable," 39, 44-45
The Gift of Death, 3
Gutmann's failure to address, 68
Habermas on, 6
"Hospitality," 136
impossibility of getting right, 17
interview with Nancy, 69-71
involvement of in French educational policy, 120
Levinas on, 82
in modern traditions, 51-52
Monolingualism of the Other, 134-35
obituary for, 1
opposition to, 11n6, 43
opposition to honorary degree for, 4-5, 43, 65
The Other Heading, 7
Paper Machine, 54
"Plato's Pharmacy," 23
Points...Interviews, 1974-1994, 43-44
as political philosopher, 6, 7, 40
Politics of Friendship, 7
The Post Card, 126
as private ironist, 121, 122
as profound humanist, 51-52

public interest in, 39, 42
reading of Nietzsche, 50
response to Cambridge Affair, 5
response to Rorty's criticisms, 124, 125
Rorty on, 6-8, 42, 122-24
Specters of Marx, 7, 41, 72
"Structure, Sign and Play in the Discourse of the Humanities," 60
as teacher, 46-47
"The Time of a Thesis," 124
"To Forgive," 39
translating, 19
writing about, 16-17, 19
writing of, 17, 27
Derrida Downunder (conference), 39
"Derrida's Last Conference" (Nigro), 4
Descombes, Vincent, 68
dialectical materialist logic, economy of, 40
dichotomies, inside/outside, 126, 127
différance, 26-27, 66, 90, 92
difference, 25-26, 90, 127
discipleship, 109
Dissemination (Derrida), 23
dogmatism, critical, 83, 84-85
Donato, Eugenio, 60

Eagleton, Terry, 3
Ecce Homo (Nietzsche), 50
The Economist, 3
economy of dialectical materialist logic, 40
economy of writing, 40
education
    closure of, 100-103
    and concern for incoming of other, 16
    critique in, 82
    curriculum, 66-67
    deconstructive nature of, 106
    dependence upon interpretations, 106
    distinction with socialization, 103
    humanist foundations of, 101-3
    inventionalism's importance for, 104
    and Kant, 99-100
    link with human freedom, 100

and literature, 126
need to prepare for incalculable, 35
problem with humanism in, 102-3
and psychological development, 100
purpose of, 98
qualification function of, 98
and rational autonomy, 99-100
rationale for, 99-100
relation with deconstruction, 33-34
relation with justice, 34
and self-determination, 100
as socialization, 98, 101, 103
and subjectification, 99, 100
transmission in, 104-5, 108, 109
education, just, 35
egology, 28
empiricism, logical, 43
"The End of Postmodernism?" (conference), 42
The End of Work (Rifkin), 117
"The Ends of Man" (Derrida), 44, 61, 63
Engel, Paschal, 65-66
Enlightenment
  alliance with colonialism, 52-53
  and freedom, 103
  Kant in, 99
Ennis, Robert, 82-83
ethicopolitical horizon of deconstruction, 15
ethics, 29, 34-35, 135
Eurocentrism, 52, 54
Europe, responsibility of for post-globalization, 54-55
exchange, 137
exclusion
  and communication, 18
  Derrida's experience with, 134-35
existentialism, 51
"Expeditions of an Untimely Man" (Nietzsche), 115
experience, link with language, 86

Falwell, Jerry, 48
Ferry, Luc, 59-60, 63-64, 65, 68, 76n6
"forgiveness," Derrida on, 44-46
"Forgiving the Unforgivable" (Derrida), 39, 44-45
Foucault, Michel, 63, 70, 102, 103

foundations, 84, 87
freedom
  and education, 100
  and Enlightenment, 103
French Philosophy of the Sixties. See *La pensée 68* (Ferry and Renaut)
Freud, Sigmund, 61
fundamentalism, 48-49

The Gay Science (Nietzsche), 49
The Gift of Death (Derrida), 3
globalization
  cosmopolitanism within context of, 134
  and end of literature, 126
  See also post-globalization; worldization
"God is dead," 49
grammatological classroom, 110
Grant, Robert, 48
Guardian, 3
Gutmann, Amy, 66-68

Habermas, Jürgen, 6, 123
Hegel, Georg W.F.
  criticism of transcendental philosophy, 85
  on critique, 82
  Derrida on reading of, 41
Heidegger, Martin
  Being and Time, 71
  Dasein concept of, 61, 70-71
  on desirability of humanism, 102
  as humanist, 71-72
  interpretation of "God is dead," 49
  man in thought of, 62
  principle of reason, 120
  reading of Nietzsche, 44, 49, 50
  relevance of to quest for justice, 122-23
  Rorty on, 121
  vestige of metaphysics in work of, 8, 44
hieroglyph, 110
Hindness, Barry, 42
history, role in twentieth-century philosophy, 82

hospitality
    in context of cosmopolitanism, 136–37
    Derrida's concept of, 134, 136–37
    Derrida's seminar on, 133
    significance of for Derrida, 135–36
"Hospitality" (Derrida), 136
Houdebine, Jean-Louis, 40
human, Kant's definition of, 100
humanism
    attempts to renew humanistic scholarship, 52–55
    challenges to, 102
    and colonialism, 53
    continuance of, 52
    deepening of, 49
    Derrida's engagement with question of, 52
    desirability of, 102
    in education, 101–3
    existentialism as, 51
    of Heidegger, 71–72
    of Levinas, 71–72
    Levinas's explanation of, 101
    and positing of norm of being human, 102–3
    possibility of, 102
    rejection of by postwar French philosophy, 63
    Said on, 53
    and socialization, 103
humanism, Christian, 51
Humanism and Democratic Criticism (Said), 53
humanities
    American debate on, 51
    attempts to renew humanistic scholarship, 52–55
    Derrida's tasks for, 117–19
    links to university without conditions, 116–17
    literature in, 118
    professor in, 118–19
    struggle over interpretation of Nietzsche in, 50
human nature, 48
Husserl, Edmund, 70

identity, 27
Inoperative Community (Nancy), 71
inside/outside dichotomies, 126, 127
institution/institutions
    literature as, 124
    Nietzsche on, 115
    philosophy as, 11n4
International, new, 74
International Collège of Philosophy, 11n6, 120
International Colloquium on Critical Languages and the Sciences of Man (conference), 60
Internationalization, 128–29
international law, 74–75, 118
interpretations, 105, 106
    See also misunderstanding
interviews given by Derrida, 43–44, 69–71
invention, 16, 110, 111
inventionalism, 16, 104
ironist, contrast with metaphysician, 122
Irvine, University of California at, 2, 47
Islam, fundamentalism in, 48

Jewishness, Derrida's, 134
Johnson, Barbara, 9
Judaism, fundamentalism in, 48
justice
    aporia of, 32–33
    Derrida's relevance to quest for, 122–23
    as directed toward the other, 31, 103
    distinction with law, 32
    Heidegger's relevance to quest for, 122–23
    impossibility of, 31–32
    relation with deconstruction, 34, 103
    relation with education, 34

Kandell, Jonathan, 1
Kant, Immanuel
    and closure of education, 100–101
    cosmopolitanism of, 136–37
    on critique, 82
    definition of human, 100
    and education, 99–100
    in Enlightenment, 99
    Perpetual Peace, 136

and task of philosophy, 85
knowledge
    and community of communication, 86
    distinction with belief, 81-82

Lacan, Jacques, 69, 70
language
    argumentative use of, 87
    difference in, 25-26
    in fundamentalism, 48
    link with experience, 86
    misunderstanding as part of, 18
    risk in, 106, 107
    Saussure's theory of, 25-26
    as writing first, 24, 25
language game, transcendental, 86
law, 32
law, international, 74-75, 118
law of singularity, 29
Lawrence, Karen, 2
learning
    gap with teaching, 107
    grammatological classroom, 110
    teaching's interaction with, 105
Le Goff, Jacques, 117
Levinas, Emmanuel
    definition of justice, 103
    on Derrida, 81
    on humanism, 101, 102
    as humanist, 71-72
    influence on Derrida, 135
    on other, 28-29
Levinasian reversal, 28-29
Levine, Peter, 50
Lévi-Strauss, Claude, 61
liberals, alliance against post-structuralism by, 65
life, human, 72
Lilla, Mark, 64, 76n6
literalism in fundamentalism, 48
literature
    as act of education, 121
    Bloom's conception of, 51
    centrality of, 121
    and democracy, 125-26
    and higher education, 126
    as institution, 125

in new humanities, 118
philosophy's links to, 44
as public, 124, 125
in public/private distinction, 125
logocentrism
    deconstruction of, 23, 27
    in metaphysical theory of meaning, 24
    need to break free from, 44
Lyotard, Jean-François, 63, 119

Macksey, Richard, 60
Magnus, Bernd, 41
man
    in Heidegger's thought, 62
    history of, 118
    rights of, 118
Marcus, Ruth Barcan, 11n6
Marx, Karl
    on critique, 82
    Derrida on reading of, 41
Marxism
    collapse of, 63
    Derrida's relationship to, 40-41
    interrogation of universalism of Enlightenment by, 63
matter, 41
meaning, 24, 51
media and democracy, 73, 74
metaphysician, contrast with ironist, 122
metaphysics
    and deconstruction, 44
    deconstruction of, 30
    Derrida's desire to shake, 21-22
    desire to end, 21
    Heidegger on, 49
    impossibility of total rupture from, 21, 30, 89-90, 92
    Nietzsche's critique of, 61
    phallogocentrism in, 49
    textual status of writing of, 25
    theme of in Derrida's writing, 20-22
    vestige of in Heidegger, 8, 44
    vestige of in Nietzsche, 44
    See also philosophy, Western
metaphysics of presence, 109
Miller, J.H., 125, 126-27
misunderstanding, 18-19, 105-7

modernism, fundamentalism as reaction to, 48
modernity, 115–16, 128
Le Monde des Debats, 45
Monolingualism of the Other (Derrida), 134–35
morality
    and human nature, 48
    Nietzsche's critique of, 51
    search for foundations of, 49–50
moralizers, new, 47–48
Moral Majority, 48
Mouffe, C., 123
multiculturalism, 66
Münchhausen Trilemma, 84, 87, 89

Nancy, Jean-Luc, 69–70, 71
National Endowment for the Humanities, 51
National Socialism, 71
nation-state, decline of, 126–27
natural science, 82, 85
neoliberalism, 40, 63
New York Times, letter to, 1–2
New Zealand
    Derrida's audience in, 39, 42
    Derrida's lecture in, 44–45
Nietzsche, Friedrich
    The Anti-Christ, 50
    Beyond Good and Evil, 50, 115
    critique of metaphysics, 61
    critique of modernity, 115–16, 128
    critique of morality, 51
    Ecce Homo, 50
    as educator, 76n10
    "Expeditions of an Untimely Man," 115
    Ferry and Renaut on, 68
    The Gay Science, 49
    On the Genealogy of Morals, 50
    on institutions, 115
    interpretations of, 50
    legacy of, 50
    and question of democracy, 68–69
    reading of by Heidegger, 44, 49, 50
    Twilight of the Idols, 50, 115
    vestige of metaphysics in work of, 44
    views of democracy, 72–73

The Will to Power, 115
    See also anti-Nietzscheans
Nietzschean-Heideggerianism, critique of, 63
Nietzscheanism, Descombes on, 68
Nigro, Rachel, 4
nihilism, 3
"A Note on Hospitality" (Anidjar), 136

On Cosmopolitanism and Forgiveness (Derrida), 39
On the Genealogy of Morals (Nietzsche), 50
ontopolitopologique, 127
The Order of Things (Foucault), 63
orientalism, 52
origin, 20–21
originary translation, 109
other
    brought into private spaces, 127
    deconstruction as affirmation of, 15–16, 29, 90, 91
    and Derrida's philosophy of hospitality, 134
    encounter with, 28–29
    incoming of, 16, 104
    invention of and just education, 35
    justice as directed toward, 31, 103
    necessity for conceptualization of, 29
    recognizing alterity of, 28–29
    responsibility to, 135
    singularity of, 29
    in Western philosophy, 28
The Other Heading (Derrida), 7

Paper Machine (Derrida), 54
pardon, 45–46
pedagogy, Derrida's, 8
pedagogy, grammatological, 110
pedagogy, new, 109–10
La pensée 68 (Ferry and Renaut), 59–60, 63–64
performative acts, 119
performative consistency, 87, 92
performative contradictions, 87, 88
Perpetual Peace (Kant), 136
Peters, M.A., 40
Phaedrus (Plato), 23
phallogocentrism, 49

philosopher
   Derrida on, 128
   distinction with common man, 82
philosopher, political, Derrida as, 6, 7, 40
philosophers, analytic, 4-5, 43
philosophize, right to, 46
philosophy
   Derrida on, 128
   as institution, 11n4
   as kind of dying, 2
   links to literature, 44
   and natural science, 82, 85
   questions of style in, 5
   resistance to Derrida, 4-5
   Wittgenstein on, 11n4
philosophy, critical, 81-82
philosophy, French, 61-62, 63-64
philosophy, transcendental, 85-88
philosophy, Western
   as attempt to locate fundamental
      ground, 20-21
   critique in, 81-82
   inability of to recognize alterity of
      other, 28
   logocentrism of, 44
   See also metaphysics
philosophy of 1960s, 59-60, 63-64
philosophy of university, post-Nietzschean, 116
phonocentrism, 23
Plato, 23, 81-82
Platonism, repudiation of, 44
"Plato's Pharmacy" (Derrida), 23
Points...Interviews, 1974-1994 (Derrida), 43-44
Politics of Friendship (Derrida), 7
Popper, Karl, 88
The Post Card (Derrida), 126
postcolonial theory, 52
post-globalization, Europe's responsibility for, 54-55
postmodernism, alleged effects of, 51
post-structuralism, 65, 69, 70
Pourquoi nous ne sommes pas nietzschéens (Ferry and Renaut), 65
pragmatics, transcendental, 86
pragmatism, 122
presence, 21, 22, 27

presence, metaphysics of, 109
presentation, 108
private
   Derrida as, 121, 122-23, 124
   distinction with public, 123, 125
profession, 117, 118
professor, 119
public, 123, 124, 125
public policy, 48

qualification function of education, 98
Questioning God (Derrida), 39
Quine, W.V.O., 43

rational autonomy, 99-100
Raynaud, Phillippe, 76n10
reason, role of in twentieth-century philosophy, 82
referent, 24
reflexivity of deconstruction, 30
Reinhard, Kenneth, 1
relativism, alleged effects of, 51
Renaut, Alain, 59-60, 63-64, 65, 68, 76n6
representation, 43, 108-9
research, politics of, Derrida on, 120
response, 20, 28
responsibility, 72
Reynolds, Jack, 135
Rifkin, Jeremy, 117
right to philosophize, 46
Rorty, Richard
   account of deconstruction, 121
   Achieving Our Country, 7
   on comparison with Derrida, 42
   Contingency, Irony, and Solidarity, 122-24
   Deconstruction and Pragmatism, 124
   on democracy, 123
   on Derrida, 6-8, 121, 122-24
   on Heidegger, 121

sacrifice of human life, 72
Said, Edward, 52-53
Sartre, Jean-Paul, 51, 61
Saussure, Ferdinand de, 25-26, 27
Scarpetta, Guy, 40
science, natural, 82, 85

Scruton, Roger, 3
Searle, John, 11n6
self, undermining of traditional ideas of, 127
self-determination, 100
self-presence, 61
self-sacrifice, 3
seminars by Derrida, 2, 47, 133
sign, 24
signified
    decentering of, 61
    in metaphysical theory of meaning, 24
signifier, 24
singularity, law of, 29
Smith, Barry, 65
socialization, 98, 101, 103
Socrates, 2, 81
sovereignty, deconstruction of concept of, 118
Specters of Marx (Derrida), 7, 41, 72
speech, assignment of truth to, 23
speech act theory, Austin's, 105
Strauss, Leo, 50
structure, 27, 60-61
"Structure, Sign and Play in the Discourse of the Humanities" (Derrida), 60
subject
    alleged lack of in post-structuralism, 65, 70
    Althusser on, 69, 70
    critique of, 63
    decentering of, 61
    Derrida accused of liquidating, 62
    Derrida's discussion of in Nancy interview, 69-70
    Foucault on, 70
    Lacan on, 69, 70
    reconstruction of, 69
subject, sovereign, Derrida's questioning of, 62
subjectification, 99, 100
subjectivity
    arguments against, 103
    inventionalism's approach to, 104
    questioning of Heideggerian critique of, 64

Taylor, Charles, 66
teacher, Derrida as, 2, 46-47
teaching
    as faithful transmission, 108, 109
    gap with learning, 107
    grammatological classroom, 110
    interaction with learning, 105
    metaphysics of presence in, 109
    politics of, Derrida on, 120
    presentation in, 108
    representation in, 108-9
technology
    and democracy, 73-74
    and end of literature, 126-27
    and inside/outside dichotomies, 126-27
telecommunications and end of literature, 126-27
thesis, Derrida's, 124-25
thinking, critical, 82-83
"The Time of a Thesis" (Derrida), 124
Times (London), 3, 4
"To Forgive" (Derrida), 39
tradition, break with, 115
transcendental critique, 83, 85-88, 92-93
transcendental language game, 86
transcendental philosophy, 85-88
translating Derrida, 19
translation
    as form of Internationalization, 129
    as a response, 20
translation, originary, 109
transmission in education, 104-5, 108, 109
Treatise on Critical Reason (Albert), 84
Trifonas, Peter, 40
truth, assignment of to speech, 23
Twilight of the Idols (Nietzsche), 50, 115
'Two Dogmas of Empiricism' (Quine), 43

Ulmer, Gregory, 108-11
The Unavowable Community (Blanchot), 71
understanding, relationship with misunderstanding, 18-19
university
    crises in, 120
    export of, 130
    indigenization of, 130

literalizing of, 120–21
and literature, 126
professionalism of, 120
university, indigenous, 130
university, post-Nietzschean philosophy of, 116
university, unconditional, 40, 116–20
urgency, aporia of, 34

violence, transcendental, 29
violence and humanism, 102
voice, privileging of, 22–24

war and humanism, 102
Warminski, Andrzej, 2
Weber, Samuel, 1
Who Comes After the Subject? (Nancy), 69
Willard, Dallas, 65
will to power, 44
The Will to Power (Nietzsche), 115
Wittgenstein, Ludwig, 11n4, 119
work, 117
worldization, 117
    See also globalization
writing
    language as, 24, 25
    privileging of voice over, 22–24
    and risk of misunderstanding, 18
    as subversive, 22
writing, Derrida's, 17, 27
writing, economy of, 40
writing about Derrida, 16–17, 19

ABOUT THE AUTHORS

Michael A. Peters (mpet001@uiuc.edu) is Professor of Education at the University of Illinois at Urbana-Champaign. He completed his Bachelor's degree in English literature and an honors degree in geography, before attaining a teaching diploma and thereafter teaching in New Zealand high schools for seven years, the last two as head of department. While teaching, he completed a major for a Bachelor of Science in philosophy and returned full time to complete his Master's degree in philosophy, with first class honors, and a Ph.D. in philosophy of education, with a thesis on the philosopher Ludwig Wittgenstein. He has just completed a second book on the subject entitled *Wittgenstein as Pedagogical Philosopher* (2008) with Nicholas C. Burbules and Paul Smeyers. He has held a personal chair at the University of Auckland (2000–2003) and was Research Professor at the University of Glasgow (2000–2005), as well as numerous posts as adjunct and visiting professor throughout the world. He is the executive editor of *Educational Philosophy and Theory* and editor of two international e-journals, *Policy Futures in Education* and *E-Learning*, and sits on the editorial board of over fifteen international journals. He has written over thirty-five books and three hundred articles and chapters, including, most recently, the following: *Global Citizenship Education* (with H. Blee & A. Britton, 2008), *Global Knowledge Cultures* (with C. Kapitzke, 2007), *Subjectivity and Truth: Foucault, Education and the Culture of Self* (2007), *Why Foucault? New Directions in Educational Research* (with T. Besley, 2007), *Building Knowledge Cultures: Educational and Development in the Age of Knowledge Capitalism* (with T. Besley, 2006), and *Knowledge Economy, Development and the Future of the University* (2007). He has strong research interests in distributed knowledge systems, digital scholarship, and e-learning systems and has acted as an advisor to government on these and related matters in Scotland, New Zealand, South Africa, and the E.U.

Gert Biesta (www.gertbiesta.com) is Professor of Education at the Stirling Institute of Education at the University of Stirling, Scotland, and Visiting Professor for Education and Democratic Citizenship at Örebro University and Mälardalen University, Sweden. He conducts theoretical and empirical research and is particularly interested in the relationships between education, democracy, and democratization. He has published on the philosophy and methodology of educational research; relationships between research, policy, and practice; theories of education; democratic learning in everyday settings; vocational education and lifelong learning; teachers' professional learning; and the civic role of Higher Education. His recent books include *Derrida & Education* (coedited with Denise Egéa-Kuehne, 2001), *Pragmatism and Educational Research* (with Nicholas C. Burbules, 2003), *Beyond Learning: Democratic Education for a Human Future* (2006), *Improving Learning Cultures in Further Education* (with David James, 2007), *Democracy, Education and the Moral Life* (coedited with Michael Katz & Susan Verducci, 2008), and *Contexts, Communities and Networks* (coedited with Richard Edwards & Mary Thorpe, 2008).

Studies in the Postmodern Theory of Education

General Editors
Joe L. Kincheloe & Shirley R. Steinberg

Counterpoints publishes the most compelling and imaginative books being written in education today. Grounded on the theoretical advances in criticalism, feminism, and postmodernism in the last two decades of the twentieth century, Counterpoints engages the meaning of these innovations in various forms of educational expression. Committed to the proposition that theoretical literature should be accessible to a variety of audiences, the series insists that its authors avoid esoteric and jargonistic languages that transform educational scholarship into an elite discourse for the initiated. Scholarly work matters only to the degree it affects consciousness and practice at multiple sites. Counterpoints' editorial policy is based on these principles and the ability of scholars to break new ground, to open new conversations, to go where educators have never gone before.

For additional information about this series or for the submission of manuscripts, please contact:

> Joe L. Kincheloe & Shirley R. Steinberg
> c/o Peter Lang Publishing, Inc.
> 29 Broadway, 18th floor
> New York, New York 10006

To order other books in this series, please contact our Customer Service Department:

> (800) 770-LANG (within the U.S.)
> (212) 647-7706 (outside the U.S.)
> (212) 647-7707 FAX

Or browse online by series:
> www.peterlang.com

www.ingramcontent.com/pod-product-compliance
Lightning Source LLC
Chambersburg PA
CBHW050123020526
44112CB00035B/2370